ETHICS AND HIDDEN GREED

Praise for *Ethics and Hidden Greed*

I find the argument in this book highly interesting. It may apply to the general public, or find use in academic environments.

Most commercial enterprises engage in greedy and unethical tactics – knowingly or unknowingly. This text is seminal work in understanding the evolution of commercial greed, its sources, root causes, and even intergenerational sources. The authors focus on the often-unethical methods, tactics, and traps deployed by commercial enterprises to seize excess rent from unsuspecting buyers. The book casts sunshine on less-than-ethical behaviors by applying the Cambridge Utilitarianism ethical approach and a clear framework which also addresses soulless technologies such as AI and powerful tech monopolies. This offers buyers insight and countertactics to avoid being cheated.

Finally, it shows why unethical strategies are ultimately value debasing.

**Professor Raul L. Katz,
Columbia University, New York.**

The world continues to change, raising questions about ethics, which perhaps we do not even know to ask. This provocative book reminds us, especially those whose faith leads them to seek a just society, to constantly keep vigil in the emerging corporate and technological world.

The Rev Richard Witt, Executive Director, Rural & Migrant Ministry. Former Chaplain at Vassar College. In 2022 Richard was named by the City and State of New York as one of its top 100 faith leaders.

Most commercial enterprises sometimes deploy greedy and unethical tactics – knowingly or unwittingly. This text is inspiring work in understanding the evolution of commercial greed, its sources, root causes, and even intergenerational sources. The authors focus on the often-unethical methods, tactics, and traps deployed by commercial enterprises to seize excess rent from unsuspecting buyers. The book casts sunshine on less-than-ethical behaviors by providing examples and a clear framework. This offers buyers insight and counter-tactics to avoid being cheated.

This work helps to find the path between ethical and strategically sound tactics and those that are short term and unethical. It shows why unethical strategies are ultimately value debasing. That is true increasingly as soulless technologies such as AI and powerful tech monopolies fall into the heavy gravitational pull of greed. As a result, ethical leadership is needed more than ever.

**Daniel E. Aks, President and CEO, Undertone, Inc.
before that, Chairman and CEO, Antenna International.**

Unethical and greedy behavior can be found in the market, and within companies.

I have found that many companies are not aware of all material unethical behavior by employees, until it becomes a legal liability. This book shows how to spot unethical behaviors which have evolved to be less obvious, and so harder to detect. This is requisite knowledge for attorneys – and particularly corporate counsel. Finally, the authors have shown how classic ethics are a tool which can go beyond legal guidelines and result in fairer, more profitable and humane practices. A must-read.

**Bruce Cranner, Partner at Talley, Anthony,
Hughes and Knight, Member of the Louisiana Bar,
Board Member, Louisiana Association of Defense,**

Federation of Defense and Corporate Counsel, Hearing Officer for Louisiana Board of Dentistry. Former Board Member National Foundation for Judicial Excellence.

The authors have surveyed the evolution of two important technologies: Artificial Intelligence and Virtual Reality, in sufficient depth to identify some of the potential ethical and criminal threats posed. The book applies traditional rules of ethics to form a weapon against (sometimes covert) unethical and criminal threats to corporate governance.

Pritish Purohit, Group Head of Information Security at NinjaVan (Singapore).

This book ties together practical advice with ethical and organizational psychology. The authors outline how forms of greed drive behavior, and how different titles within a company have very different motivations: some are there to grow revenues, others are there to defend the company from financial and ethical misbehavior. Well worth a look for any CFO or manager who wants to uphold ethical standards.

Julio Zamora, Chief Financial Officer, North American Development Bank.

ETHICS AND HIDDEN GREED

Your Defense Against Unethical Strategies and Violations of Trust

BY

ROB DOCTERS
And

HANS GIESKES

United Kingdom – North America – Japan
India – Malaysia – China

Emerald Publishing Limited
Howard House, Wagon Lane, Bingley BD16 1WA, UK

First edition 2023

Reprints and permissions service
Contact: permissions@emeraldinsight.com

British Library Cataloguing in Publication Data
A catalogue record for this book is available from the British Library

ISBN: 978-1-80455-871-3 (Print)
ISBN: 978-1-80455-868-3 (Online)
ISBN: 978-1-80455-870-6 (Epub)

ISOQAR certified
Management System,
awarded to Emerald
for adherence to
Environmental
standard
ISO 14001:2004.

Certificate Number 1985
ISO 14001

INVESTOR IN PEOPLE

TABLE OF CONTENTS

Section V: Ethical Strategy

Section VI: Ethical Leadership

LIST OF TABLES AND FIGURES

Chapter 12

Chapter 13

ABOUT THE AUTHORS

Rob Docters is the lead author of *Ethics and Hidden Greed*.

He has held senior positions in consulting, industry, and academia. Consulting experience includes:

- Head of Asia Enablement Center, and Pricing Team, Boston Consulting Group, in Singapore.

- Senior Vice President at Ernst & Young, and Co-Leader of the Toronto strategy practice.

- Senior Expert, McKinsey and Company, in New York, and

- Principal at Booz, Allen and Hamilton, Inc., in New York.

Corporate experience includes:

- Head of New Market Innovation, Bloomberg LLP,

- Senior Vice President of Strategy, Business Development, and Pricing at LexisNexis, and

- Executive Head of Revenue Growth, Reed Exhibitions.

Educational and professional credentials Include:

- A.B. Stanford University, 1979 (Economics); J. D. The College of William and Mary, School of Law (1982); M. B. A. Columbia University, School of Business (1984)

- Member, New York Bar

- Lecturer in Management, Yale University, School of Management (2017 and 2018). Taught courses as part of the marketing core. He has also taught at the National University of Singapore.

Rob is the primary author of two influential books on pricing strategy: *Contextual Pricing* and *Winning the Profit Game*, which were published in the United States, Germany, Norway, and China. These books are assigned as supplementary texts at several leading universities. He has authored over 24 articles for peer-reviewed publications, including the groundbreaking "Pricing as a Language" in the *Journal of Business Strategy*, and *EMBA*.

Rob is a competitive yachtsman, and lives with his wife and dog. His email address is RDocters@AbbeyLLP.com.

Hans Gieskes is coauthor of *Ethics and Greed.*

Hans has been turn-around CEO and Chairman of companies in a range of industries, such as information services, publishing, and data and professional services.

Relevant professional experiences include:

- LexisNexis Group. President and CEO

- Houghton Mifflin Publishing Co. (Boston). Chairman and CEO

- Elsevier (London and Amsterdam). CEO Elsevier UK and EVP roles at Elsevier Group

- Cision.com Group (Stockholm). CEO

- Monster.com (Boston). President

- OneOcean.com Group (London). Chairman

- AXIO Data Group. (London). Chairman

- Non-Executive Director for a dozen VC backed start-ups and other companies

- Leadership involvement in 30 major M&A transactions worldwide, two of which greater are than $1.6B

Educational Credentials Include:

- Netherlands Institute for Marketing, BA (1982)
- Henley Management College – The Senior Course (1988)

Other:

- Honorary Consul for Kingdom of The Netherlands

Hans and his wife spend their time in Boston, MA, upstate NY, and Hilton Head Island SC

ACKNOWLEDGMENTS

The authors would like to thank and acknowledge the contributions of: Nancy Lothrop, Leonie Gieskes, Stephen Lipton, Gordon Daily, Pritish Purohit, Bruce Cranner, Pam Docters, Bill Moran, Vicky Baker, Peter Garand, Mr Muffin, Ade van Duyn, Dan Aks, Martijn Gieskes, Julio Zamora, Dan Jansenson, Michael Barzelay, Mark Nevins, J. M. Izaret, Paul Brown, Petra Recter, Larry Oliver, Patrick Thiede, Phebe Prescott, Ursula Moran, Linda Sullivan, Gayle Maurin, Meryl Moss, and Kirsty Woods. These individuals all offered new insight and corrections.

SECTION I

INTRODUCTION

INTRODUCTION – WHAT TO EXPECT OF THIS BOOK

Question: Will this book involving ethics have utility in the real world?

This book takes a different approach to be more useful to readers. It does not spend much time discussing the differences among different schools of ethics. This is because the ethical answers to important real-world questions are quite similar, whether you are talking about Cambridge Utilitarians, Immanuel Kant, or Aristotle. To the extent there are differences, those differences lie more in their bases and supporting logic than their conclusions or rationales. For instance, all schools agree that using deception to prevail in negotiations is unethical. Further, most schools of ethics agree that you should treat others as you yourself want to be treated. There are differences (usually intuitive) on how these rules emerged and their foundation, but not in the recommended actions.

Based on this similarity, we have chosen to focus on one school's principles and run with it. We use the Cambridge Neoplatonist School, as articulated by Professor Henry More, a Cambridge ethicist and guiding light. Its rules are laid out in a pretty straightforward fashion and are not controversial. We have chosen his list of 23 principles – or "Noema" – as a guide. These can be found in the appendix, translated from the Latin. We take the principles as a given. What will not be found in this book is an advanced discussion of the merits of these principles. That is a different book. We did not see a need for it. We suspect readers won't either.

By way of background, a few words about Professor More. *Encyclopaedia Britannica* assessed him as someone who "can never be spoken of, however, save as a spiritual genius and a significant figure in British philosophy. Further the chief feature of his character [was] a certain radiancy of thought which carried him beyond the common life without raising him to any artificial height, for his humility and charity were conspicuous..."[1]

Indeed, Professor More repeatedly declined honors and promotions, including, in 1654, Mastership of Christ's College, Cambridge. Professor More's *Enchiridion Ethicum*, his treatise on ethics and moral values, is the foundation of our book. His goal was to uphold the "essential and eternal distinction of good and evil." Based on the "intellectual force of the soul by which... the 'sweetness and flavor' of virtuous conduct is manifest."[2]

While basing this book on Professor More's writings, we do borrow from Kant, as needed. For instance, our chapter on artificial reality would be difficult to write without considering the *intent* of developers.

So, you might ask, why is this book valuable? This book will provide ethical prescriptions and frequently a strategy for recognizing and dealing with ethical issues confronting you and society at large. The issues are myriad. For instance, how have labels on consumer goods, food and various packaged goods been twisted so they are no longer accurate? What music are you allowed to reproduce, and why? How does one respond to assault by unethical people? How does a person remain ethical while defending against the unethical? What are the ethics in the world of artificial reality? What are the ethics of intergenerational conflict – a serious question when dealing with issues such as environmental calamity or college debt? What are legitimate societal ethical grievances? What serious ethical misdeeds are being ignored by society at this time?

Comparing the "World's Most Ethical Companies" survey to the S&P 500 over time suggests that ethical behavior is rewarded. The most ethical companies outperform other companies by 7.1%

---

[1]More, Henry, Encyclopedia Britannica, 11th Edition, Vol. XVIII, p. 822.
[2]H. Sidgwick, *Outlines of the History of Ethics*, Macmillan, 1896, pp. 172–173.

over a 15-year period.[3] There is considerable evidence that ethical behavior improves customer relationships."[4] Ethics are the antecedent building block to the establishment of trust and loyalty.

This book will help people recognize and defend against unethical actions. A cornerstone to any successful defense requires learning how to identify unethical strategies and how they may evade detection. This book contains hundreds of examples of unethical strategies. While detection can be difficult, it is critically important. You will learn how to recognize them. Further, the application of More's clear rules can show that some actions casually assumed to be unethical (e.g., making a lot of money) are not unethical (although they may be ethically hazardous). Also, even more surprising, often the "victims" as seen through an unsophisticated lens are actually the unethical players!

Unlike some books on ethics, this book will provide an answer to many (but far from all) ethical dilemmas. This book digs into the details of many gritty but important questions. Once the fact set is clear, ethical permutations are sharply reduced and the result is clarity. This book differs from ethical texts which tread lightly on the facts and are often vague because of numerous doctrinal differences. While these quibbles are legitimate, the eventual answers are about the same. More often, these quibbles result in a circular rather than direct approach to an answer. Once you have a basic answer, refinements are always possible and always easier to come by – our intent is to provide an ethical life jacket for survival, not a guide to the ethical fine wines in the ship's bar.

This book also is different in that it considers ethical issues from both the point of view of individuals as well as from the point of view of a business manager. This provides the most germane guidance. After all, many humans occupy both roles. Understanding both roles helps one to navigate to an ethical life (Fig. I.1).

---

[3]Ethisphere Institute "2021 World's Most Ethical Companies" Recognition Program, *Ethisphere*, February 23, 2021.
[4]Linda F. Thornton, "Ethics and Trust are Reciprocal," Leading in Context, June 18, 2014. Also O. Ferrell, J. Fraedrich and L. Ferrell, *Business Ethics* (11th Edition), Cengage Learning 2017, p. 16.

Ethics, Morals and Law Interact

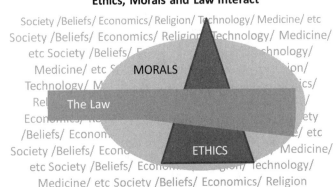

Society /Beliefs/ Economics/ Religion/ Technology/ Medicine/ etc
Society /Beliefs/ Economics/ Religion/ Technology/ Medicine/
etc Society /Beliefs/ ... ... hnology/
Medicine/ etc ... ... ion/
Technology/ M ... ... ics/
Rel ... The Law ... /
Eco ... ... ety
/Beliefs/ Econom ... /etc
Society /Beliefs/ Econo ... ETHICS ... Medicine/
etc Society /Beliefs/ Eco ... echnology/
Medicine/ etc Society /Beliefs/ Economics/ Religion

MORALS

Fig. I.1. Ethics, Moral, and Law Interact.

Finally, this book blends ethics, morals, and law. These three bodies of rules influence each other and often where one leaves off, the other begins.

This matters because societal issues and challenges often intersect all three categories of rules. Professor More begins his book by declaring "Ethicks are defined to be the Art of Living well and happily." This immediately distinguishes it from much of law and, to some extent, morals. Each of the three can stand alone – some laws (like traffic or tax laws) have no moral or ethical basis.[5] Some moral principles (like risking one's life for a loved one) have no ethical basis. Finally, ethics can stand independent of both law and morals.[6]

This book should also form the basis for new questions. The authors were surprised when rigorously examining case examples showed that often the "victim" of unethical actions is often guilty of ethical infractions also. These infractions are not necessarily as serious, but worth a look. If both sides are at fault, is it harder to assign ethical responsibility?[7]

---

[5]W. Starr, "Law and Morality in H.L.A. Hart's Legal Philosophy",
Marquette Law Review, Summer 1984, Article 8.
[6]Chapter I, Section I.
[7]As an analogy, in the law, states are divided between those which attempt to allocate blame (and damages) among the parties. This is called "comparative" negligence, while some others refuse to do so, and look for "contributory" negligence. Comparative negligence is the majority practice.

Finally, we encourage readers to dive into the topics or chapters which are most important to you. The priority of topics is, of course, up to you.

In this book we often quote Professor More, who uses the term "Noema." That word may be unfamiliar. A Noema is "an act or decision based on considered thought." And it represents guidance for ethical decision-makers.

SECTION II

HIDDEN GREED

1

GREED AND STEALTH

Question: Do you recognize greed and ethical challenges?

Don't let my white duds and pleasant demeanor fool ya.
I have been known to violate the statutes of men and
not a few of the rules of the Almighty.

The Ballad of Buster Scruggs, a film by Joel and Ethan
Coen

AN EVOLUTION

About 700 years ago, in Medieval England, there lived a baker. At that time, bread was sold by weight, so like other bakers, he would weigh dough in front of customers to show they were getting their money's worth. This was a time of cheap labor and expensive materials. To combat the high cost of ingredients, this baker had a boy hidden under the counter who, after the dough was weighed and placed on the counter, would open a secret trapdoor and remove a handful of dough before it was placed in the oven.

This improved the baker's return on investment (ROI) quite nicely.

Sadly, for the greedy baker, he was discovered. As this was also a time of harsh punishments, the baker was flogged, paraded through the streets, and hung.[1]

Fast-forward to the twentieth century. Despite the evolution of technology and the many improvements in our lives, the baker's trick of taking back what has been sold is still around. But the contexts are different. For instance, Apple Computer was recently criticized for exactly that sort of conduct. Expert iPhone users discovered that Apple was slowing down the speed of older models of iPhone. Some argued this was a strategy designed to induce users to upgrade to newer and more expensive iPhones.[2] Apple claimed this was an effort to save battery draw, but notably, the company did not reveal that fact until users detected the speed loss.

Was this an example of greed on Apple's part? That judgment depends on how much trust you have in Apple. While Apple later announced a substantial reduction in replacement battery prices to offset the change in speeds, this did not defuse the complaints. If Apple had thought about the problem, it could have done better. For one thing, it could have avoided a "naked" (obvious) obser-vation: A simultaneous announcement that of battery price change as an offset to the change in speed might have been perceived as a fair move.

TRANSACTION TERMS

Why are term changes, such as speeds of iPhones, important in commerce? It is important because terms and price make up the formula of give and take – the ratio of goods and services provided divided by dollars demanded. The money price means nothing without knowing the goods or services associated with that price.

---

[1]Mary Ellen Fitzroy, *Encyclopedia of Kitchen History* (Fitzroy Dearborn, NY 2004), p. 49.
[2]"Apple has been fined 25 million euros (£21m, $27m) for deliberately slowing down older iPhone models without making it clear to consumers," *BBC News*, February 7, 2020. The fine was imposed by France's competition and fraud watchdog DGCCRF, which said consumers were not warned. N. Hughes, "To many, Apple's admission seemed like proof of the company's grand conspiracy to force people to keep buying new phones." Appleinsider.com, December 28, 2017.

Sometimes, the money gets more attention (e.g., with a "30% Off" sale). Sometimes, the associated goods (e.g., "longer warranty") are the focus. Ethically aware managers must have an understanding and a voice on both. Otherwise, ethical standards are toothless. Unfortunately, line management frequently separates the two elements.

It is essential for managers and customers to be familiar with all the components of strategies which may lead to accusations that a company is greedy or misbehaving.

Other examples of perceived greed can be found in the telecom industry, where there have been changes in the relationship of dollars versus service offered. Classic examples include the advent of the 57-second minute and illusory bandwidth claims.

In the first example, the US telecom system, for many years, charged customers by the minutes of voice time on a call. This made sense, as talk is what you wanted to buy, not the seconds of call setup and ring time. However, a look in the files of the Federal Communications Commission (FCC) will show that most telephone companies now charge for *all* the use of their networks – including the call setup and close-down time for mobile calls. Since those components take about 3–4 seconds of each minute, effectively talk time makes up only about 57 seconds of each minute of call time. Since this is how the tariff is filed with the government, it's quite legal. As most people were unaware of this sleight of hand, the practice spread. No telecom provider wants to have to explain to its customers that its rates' quotes are higher because it does not charge for setup time – there are better marketing activities!

Similarly, internet capacity is traded among carriers and content providers. Consumers are offered specific bandwidth capacities, for example, 30 MBPS, but in fact cable companies do not always provide this capacity. They do not buy necessary additions during peak house to accommodate increased demand, so subscribers have to share split capacity, which means slower speeds.

MANY GROWTHS ("A GARDEN") OF GREED

The world has evolved since the baker came to a sticky end, and so have forms of greed. New forms of greed have grown up to take advantage of improved technology, greater product/service complexity, context, and communication.

A succinct summary of the forms of greed is our "Garden of Greed," diagrammed below in Fig. 1.1, which shows how greed has evolved to comprise a thicket of distinct tactics. The evolution reads roughly from left (early) to right (recent). While the particulars of each greedy tactic have evolved, none of the branches have, to our knowledge, disappeared. There are many minor innovations in greed and deceit; however, they are merely petals growing from each branch.

What makes the morphology interesting is that the new forms of greed can be creative, smart, and effective. Each form of greed varies in effectiveness depending on its environment. In an increasingly digital and virtual world, it appears that seizing language has become increasingly common, and so needs to be part of any ethical analysis.

Examples of the major categories of greed:

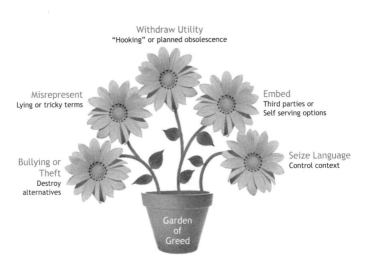

Fig. 1.1. Garden of Greed.

- *Bullying or theft* – Theft, robbery, and bullying are the most fundamental forms of taking. During the 2016 presidential campaign, the Trump Organization was accused of refusing to pay small vendors.[3] No surprise, large companies often choose to stiff vendors. As a former head of pricing at General Electric Company (GE) once commented, "It's very hard for small vendors to get any money out of GE." Governments are also good at taking. And no one should expect fairness. For instance, the state of Texas used eminent domain to seize land with a length of railroad track – rendering the remainder of the hundred-mile route inoperable. Not surprisingly, they proposed to compensate for only the short length taken.

- *Part of bullying is to destroy alternatives* – Without an alternative, buyers have little choice. An early example of this occurred in the 1940s when automobile companies bought up tramcar lines and pulled up the tracks.[4] The result? Cars were the only viable choice for those needing mechanized transportation.

- *Misrepresentation and lying* – Misrepresenting a potential purchase is an ancient practice. Hence the Roman graffito: "If fools did not go to market, cracked pots would not be sold." However, as we moved away from tangible purchase, where one

---

[3]S. Reilly, "Hundreds allege Donald Trump doesn't pay his bills," *USA Today*, June 9, 2016.

[4]On April 9, 1947, nine corporations and seven individuals (officers and directors of certain corporate defendants) were indicted in the Federal District Court of Southern California on counts of "conspiring to acquire control of a number of transit companies, forming a transportation monopoly" and "conspiring to monopolize sales of buses and supplies to companies owned by National City Lines" [38] which had been made illegal by the 1890 Sherman Antitrust Act. In 1948, the venue was changed from the Federal District Court of Southern California to the Federal District Court in Northern Illinois following an appeal to the United States Supreme Court (in *United States v. National City Lines Inc.*) [39] which felt that there was evidence of conspiracy to monopolize the supply of buses and supplies. *United States v. National City Lines*, 334 U.S. 573 (1948).

In 1949, Firestone Tire, Standard Oil of California, Phillips Petroleum, GM, and Mack Trucks were convicted of conspiring to monopolize the sale of buses and related products to local transit companies controlled by NCL; they were acquitted of conspiring to monopolize the ownership of these companies. The verdicts were upheld on appeal in 1951 [41]. GM was fined $5,000 and GM treasurer H. C. Grossman was fined $1 [42].

could examine the pot for cracks, to buying intangibles, the potential for misrepresentations has multiplied. For instance, when purchasing a financial security, one salient question is "What is the risk of loss?" In some cases, in order to win customers or market share, a seller will understate the risk of loss. Interestingly, this is particularly true when the actual returns promised are *modest*, as the low return implies low risk to many people. For instance, the Schwab "Yield Plus Select shares" advertised highly safe investments. However, when returns on those investments fell, the fund managers moved to more risky real-estate securities and incurred a staggering loss. Many investors lost much of their capital.[5] Similar losses occurred in cryptocurrency holdings when traders employed the "pump and dump" strategy to bid up values, then sold their holdings leaving lagging, less savvy, investors with shrunken values.[6]

- *Withdrawal of utility or "Hooking"* – The withdrawal of utility is different than the Apple tactic, as it is arranged ahead of time through setting a trap ("Hooking"). In this scenario, a product is divided into more than one purchase so that a buyer needs to buy a related product which the seller knows will be needed later (at additional and usually higher cost.) The viability of this strategy depends on a lack of buyer awareness and a desirable product. In that vein, car companies have struggled with what to include in warranties. Henry Ford once commented: "I would give my cars away for free, if I were guaranteed sales of the spare parts." Buyer suspicion usually means purchasers understand that the sale of spare parts is separate from the car. It is not so obvious when considering software packages. For instance, at one point, ThomsonReuters/RIA, the tax software vendor, sold its software packages without full archival facilities. Accountants who bought the package believed they were buying at bargain prices; however, when they needed archives for past

---

[5]R. Schroeder letters to investor, July–December 2008, Charles Schwab Corporation.
[6]"Crypto 'Pump and Dumps' Distorts Trading," *The Wall Street Journal*, August 6, 2018, p. B1.

taxes, they had little choice but to buy the missing archive element from ThomsonReuters – at a less competitive price.

- *Embed an agent* – An example of embedding an agent comes from the executive recruiting industry. Many clients ask, and believe, that recruiters will present the most capable candidates to management. However, as related by a partner in a top-two recruiting firm, they will exclude some classes of candidates, regardless of merit. For instance, candidates over 60 years old are usually excluded because they are not consistent with recruiting firm profit goals.

  Headhunters often make most of their money from follow-on hires, e.g., after a CEO is placed, they will typically ask the recruiter who placed them to find other senior team members. The older the CEO, the shorter the interval during which the recruiting firm has an advantaged position. Therefore, even if an older candidate has superior experience and track record, he will be passed over in favor of embedding a younger executive who can be a repeat client for many years. Not consistent with hiring committee goals, in all likelihood – but more profitable for the headhunter who enjoys more business in coming years.

- *Seize the language* – Not being able to use the right words can cripple a marketing effort. For example, the US Food and Drug Administration (FDA) has regulated the use of terms related to pharmaceutical products. This includes relatively innocuous products marketed as "suntan lotion" and "sunblock." Surprised?

  The FDA regulates the use of terms and how they may be used, freedom of speech notwithstanding. The rationale is to avoid confusion. So, in this instance, the FDA regulates which chemicals may be used in any product called sunblock or sunscreen. Coincidentally, some of those chemicals are protected by patents owned by lotion companies such as Coppertone. This is very useful because it means that only a few companies can claim to offer "sunscreen."[7] The result is very high prices for lotions which are not expensive to produce.

- *Context* – Sometimes this means taking advantage of another's situation and dire needs. The line between destroying alternatives and astute segmentation is not always clear. Knowing buyer situation can help sellers target low-alternative opportunities. In 2017, the cover of *Forbes* magazine declared: "New Billionaire David Zalik – $9 Billion in loans without a cent of risk."[8] The story described how Zalik founded a company which offered instant loan processing, so contractors could help homeowners take out loans for home improvement, usually instantly, as part of the contractor-selling process. Zalik's company got 6% of the loan amount. The actual loans were held by 14 banks, so Zalik was not the actual lender. His company did help sell the loan. The first $10,000 of the loan was interest-free for 18 months. But if the loan was not paid off in full within the 18 months, borrowers owed interest from day one. This wrinkle was not always considered by the buyers at the excited moment of decision. Greedy?

BUT, IS GREED GOOD?

The main character of the 1987 movie *Wall Street*, played by Michael Douglas, told an audience of stockholders that "Greed, for lack of a better word, is good."

Most dictionaries define greed as "extreme wanting."[9] There is no suggestion greed requires a bad act. Our review of the forms of greed suggests that a refinement to the definition of greed found in most dictionaries is in order.

---

[7] Whereas the FDA has declared only a handful of ingredients qualified to be called suntan lotion, the European Union has found that a much longer list of ingredients serve this purpose.
[8] *Forbes*, September 5, 2017, p. 62.
[9] The Oxford English Dictionary, Fourth Edition, p. 529, defines greed as "Insatiable longing, esp. for wealth."

A review of the greedy actions listed here all contains something that many observers would consider unfair or deceitful or dishonest. Or, at the very least, unkind.

This is important.

It is the distinction between greed and being competitive. For example, an extremely driven musician who seeks to surpass all other artists in his performances is competitive. An emulator of Bernie Madoff, who wants to grow an investment fund by any means, is greedy.

GREED AND PRICE STRUCTURE

Many people think that greed is related to price levels, but price structures (the way the offer is conditioned – Buy one, get one free) can be innately greedy. Price structure design is an arcane art and so may suffer from a lack of understanding and familiarity – perhaps why some price structures are prejudged by buyers as greedy. Some people believe that price level and structure should be uniform across scale and inventory ("everything should cost the same."). Yet consumers are used to nonuniform pricing. For instance, when consumers discover a publicized sale, they understand that not all inventory is on sale. Consumers also understand that not all inventory is being marked down by the same amount.

Scaling of price is a little trickier. No one is surprised that beverages are cheaper per ounce in larger bottles. Similarly, everyone understands the purpose and logic of "buy one, get one half price" and similar structures.

But suppose the scaling is not linear. Does honesty and transparency require straight lines? A top-three charge card issuer introduced a nonlinear transaction rate for merchants in Asia. The price structure sought to influence merchants accepting multiple cards to steer customers to use the charge company's card. The price break-point was based on a merchant's historical volumes. The charge company offered a sharp discount on transaction fees for volumes *above* the merchant's historical revenue levels. This led merchants, in the short term, to steer their customers to use the card which offered lower processing and interchange rates to them.

Credit Card Fee Structure

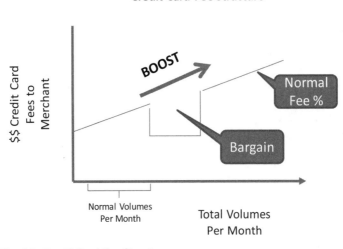

Fig. 1.2. Credit Card Fee Structure.

Then, as the merchant crossed the volume target for new business for the card, the card resumed the old (normal) rates. Often merchants did not know, real time, when they had crossed back to normal rates. So they kept steering customers to the (formerly discounted) card (Fig. 1.2).

This proved very effective in Asia, but was not rolled out in North America. Why? Concerns about merchant perception.

WHAT TO DO?

So, what can we do about greed, in whatever form it appears? There are a number of strategies which can help fend off the proponents of greedy pricing, if that is the goal.

To be clear, we are not pressing a moral agenda. It is, however, inescapable that we live in ecosystems (the "garden") which are willing to use means some would describe as greedy. It is worth noting that greed may not be a path which results in loyal customers or longer-term revenue. If you wish to thwart greedy actions, for a start you need to recognize the tactics.

- Make clear that price is a balance, a ratio of give and take. For companies, the *take* usually means the price asked, but often management manipulates the less conspicuous understanding of the *give* (the product or service) and will be tempted to provide less to the buyers. This is easy to do.

- Have advanced tools and measures to show the harm in some greedy tactics. While many managers believe their company knows the impact of pricing changes, often they are mistaken. For instance, can you describe the asymmetry in results in raising versus lowering prices? Are you aware lowering prices often requires direct communication with customers?

  Few companies or marketers have reliable links among the steps in price change. Few have really quantified the value of the good or ancillary service quality. How long does it take customers to respond when, for example, 5% of the market value of a good or service is removed, but the price is held constant? What happens after a change in price/value? What is the lifetime Net Present Value (NPV) of such a move? Without provable measures, the decision will be up to the political power within the firm, and the more ethical, long term, people may not always win.

- Make incentives include long-run results – There are many ways a smart manager with the wrong incentives can optimize for the short term, leaving chaos in following years.[10] Fortunately, there are early warning signs such as lack of candor about proposed actions.

- Monitor competitors more closely. In many competitive industries, the competitors may be the ones who will notice short-term impacts first. Their actions, if called out, may be a good early-warning signal if the market frowns. The market will often punish poor behavior – for example, creating extra customer accounts has hurt Wells Fargo,[11] and violating privacy at Facebook has led to user hesitancy.

---

[10]Cf. P. Volker, "Think more boldly." *The Wall Street Journal*, December 14, 2009.
[11]B. Eisen, Wells Fargo Reaches Settlement With Government Over Fake-Accounts Scandal, *The Wall Street Journal*, February 20, 2021.

- Preemptive ethics and transparency – This has worked well, both for signals to the market and internally. A leading soft drink company was surreptitiously sent a package containing competitor research on new products and potential pricing being undertaken by its primary competitor. The package was sent by an employee of the competitor, who offered additional confidential information. The soft drink company immediately returned the information, unread, to the competitor. The signal was clear: only open competition would be countenanced.

UNDERSTANDING GREED AND TRUST

Today's greed is less about the price tag and increasingly is more about the service or the offer. Components, quality, embedding, alternatives, and messaging/language can be manipulated less obtrusively than price tags and discounts. Of course, there will be some brute force tactics (e.g., "take"), but they are usually well understood after one instance. Familiarity with all forms of greed is important. Everyone should have a clear strategy for addressing greed – either as a consumer or as a company manager.

2

THE TORN FABRIC OF TRUST

Question: How do you preserve and build trust?

> The essence of trust building is to emphasize the similarities between you and the customer.
>
> Thomas J. Watson

On the corporate front, many companies, perhaps most, believe that building customer trust is rewarded in the market. For example, the plastic construction toymaker LEGO – ranked in the top five for trust – was able to raise prices substantially to cover the added costs of switching to eco-friendly materials because buyers believed in the company. Consequently, buyers accepted the higher prices without complaint.[1]

Some commentators have gone so far as to say that trust is "essential" for any transaction.[2] As a minor quibble, we do not believe that trust is always essential. We believe, rather, that it is helpful. An example of transactions without trust can be drawn from the siege of Stalingrad during the Second World War.

---

[1] See "How LEGO Customer Service Winds Back Upset Customers: A Simple Recovery Approach Works Wonders," Forbes.com, April 13, 2018; T. Espiner, "Why is Lego Not Clicking with Customers?" BBC News, March 6, 2018, last paragraph; V. Valet "The World's Most Reputable Companies 2019," *Forbes*, March 7, 2019.

[2] For instance, The Young Entrepreneurs Council has written articles extolling the value of trust. S. Porat, "Why Trust is a Critical Success Factor for Business Today", Forbes.com. July 7, 2017.

Veterans have recalled that even while Germans and Russians were trying to kill one another, fighting over the same building, the Germans would lower cigarettes in a pot from the upper floors. In exchange, the Russians would send up pots of water.[3]

"TRUST" HAS TWO BASES

People use only a very limited number of ways to establish trust. Sadly, however, if you wish to build trust, relying on the "usual suspects" to build trust will likely fail. Whether you seek to establish trust or wish to avoid being deceived, you must know the drivers of trust. Violated trust is a common concomitant of ethical violations. It appears that trust comes in two forms and these two flavors differ in motivation, logic, decision process, and customer verification.

After looking at more than some 175 client business models, we see customer trust can be "broad" and "narrow."[4] In the former category, there is a general belief that the other party is "good, honest, sincere."[5] In the other category, there is a narrow belief that the other party "...will do what you expect of them."[6] While these two forms of trust have some aspects in common, everyone should understand the distinction and the different requirements to build trust with each kind of audience.

Narrow Trust

In addition to the Stalingrad example, above, a form of *narrow* trust is demonstrated in the instances in which several cities and companies have had their computer systems hacked and frozen by cyber bandits demanding six- or seven-digit ransoms in cyber cash. Without any means of ensuring compliance, cities had to trust that

---

[3]Anatoliy Gigoryevich Merezhko, "Facing Stalingrad", *Berlin Journal*, Fall 2011, p. 13.
[4]Client assignments 2009–2018 at five consulting firms (Booz, Allen & Hamilton, Ernst & Young, Abbey, LLP, McKinsey & Company and BCG).
[5]"Trust," Oxford Advanced Learners Dictionary, Oxford University Press, 2020, p. 1375.
[6]Ibid.

the hackers would actually make good and release the systems.[7] Note that this required trusting someone of whom little was known except that they were criminals. In some cases, apparently, this was a good bet.[8]

Broad Trust

A well-known example of *broad* trust involves Nordstrom, a chain of department stores. In one instance, which was verified by journalists, a customer brought in automobile tires to the Fairbanks, Alaska store, and succeeded in "returning" them even though Nordstrom does not sell tires. In another instance, a Nordstrom employee found a customer's handbag in the store. Upon learning the customer was leaving on a flight, the employee drove the bag to the airport to return it to the grateful customer.[9] This speaks to a broad trustworthiness, in which customers can rely on Nordstrom to help them with not only their needs but also their failures.

Many companies fall somewhere in between these two examples. Consider online titan Twitter. This service had over 290 million active users, but made no effort to thwart predatory practices by some subscribers, another example is Apple, among the most respected companies in the world,[10] discovered that Suyin Electronics, one of its Chinese-based suppliers, relied on child labor on multiple occasions, but still took three years to fully cut purchases.[11]

---

[7]R. Siegel, "Florida City Will Pay Hackers $600,000 to Get Its Computer Systems Back," *The Washington Post*, June 20, 2019. Clearly, the city trusted the hackers to the extent that it did not see the chance of recovery as zero. See also A. Isaac, C. Ostroff and B. Hope, "Travelex Paid Hackers Ransom of $2Million Before Financial Scandal," *New York Times*, April 10, 2020, p. B1.

[8]Some readers may wonder if this is an example of trust, rather than simple optimization. Note that the value of paying the ransom is an expected value: [(value of recovered systems x probability of recovery) – Cost of payment = Payment – Any amount likely to be recovered]. The probability is purely a function of trust. If there is no trust, then the probability is zero, and there is no benefit to paying.

[9]C. Conte, "Nordstrom Customer Service Tales Are Not Just Legend," *Jacksonville Business Journal*, September 7, 2012, Food and Lifestyle section.

[10]C. Cutter, "Apple Takes Top Honors," The *Wall Street Journal*, December 3, 2019, p. R1.

[11]T. Sonnemaker, "Apple Knew It Was Using Child Labor," The Insider.com, December 31, 2020.

- Indeed, Apple ranks below the top 50 in some lists of most trustworthy companies.[12] We suspect customers admire Apple's engineering, but not necessarily its ethics.

What if your company does not happen to have a world-changing technology or similar asset? Well, then your company may need a strategy for building trust. A rough estimate from our survey of 175 companies suggests that more than half of companies, perhaps 60%, operate in markets where the broad view prevails.[13] This means customers, in effect, say "I admire company X for attributes A, B and C. I don't know much about attributes D – Z, but I will trust them based on A, B and C."

This is "associative logic." In these markets, companies need to disappoint a customer before the customer will lose confidence. That is good news for established companies, but bad news for newer ones – a lot of time and effort is required to build this kind of trust.

In contrast, some 40% of customers look specifically to factors like alignment of goals, transactional profitability, and consistency of the offer to determine whether they trust the offer. This is good news in that newcomers can establish beachheads in the market. At the same time, the bad news is that it takes more effort to retain share.

The market orientation to trust has powerful implications for business models. Broad associative logic suggests building an overall relationship, e.g., a subscription with opt-out – such as telephone services and Google. A narrower approach means relying upon transactional goods or services like the US Postal Service or fast-food giant Chick-fil-A. Some companies have successfully become hybrids, such as Amazon with its Prime program and COSTCO with its membership subscription. They know that customers will pay a fixed membership charge because customers trust that these providers will offer value in future.

Both forms of trust can translate to high loyalty and trustworthiness – they just need to be developed and used differently. Both

---

[12]V. Valet, "The World's Most Reputable Companies," *Forbes*, March 7, 2019.
[13]Estimate based survey of client markets by Abbey, LLPs, consultants 2003–2020. Supported by inference in Morning Consult, "Most Trusted Brands 2020," survey, p. 15.

forms are present in the companies which make up the top 10 trustworthy companies list. Table 2.1 highlights some of the differences. For instance, companies with broad trust resemble Mother Theresa, and those with narrow goals resemble Machiavelli.

Applicable to both kinds of trust is the basis on which buyers and parties to a transaction make their decision. Both types have a set of specific tests for trustworthiness. Even the broad decision-makers have a limited set of tests for trustworthiness. This means your company must address the right factors. Both narrow and broad require you to be "market-oriented." This means focused on what customers want, not the tools of marketing outreach.[14] Because customer decision-makers have a limited set of "litmus tests" for trustworthiness, your company must address those factors correctly. It's similar to typing in a computer password – you only need one wrong digit and the password will fail.

Table 2.1. Two Types of Trust.

Characteristic	Broad	Narrow
Perceived motivation:	Company wants to help customers	Transactional gain/avoid loss
Personification:	Mother Theresa	Machiavelli
Logic:	Associative/Emotive	Causal/Factual
Decision:	Opt out?	Opt in?
Litmus tests:	Simple and transparent Caring/nice/courteous/self-confident Consistency over time	Match to immediate goals Probability of success Consistency of offer elements External reinforcement, e.g., Relative power and risks
Basis:	Selective information or a "litmus test"	

[14]B. Shapiro, "What the Hell is 'Market Oriented?'" *Harvard Business Review*, November 1988.

LIMITED INFORMATION

The decision to trust the municipal cyber bandits was made in the narrow context of potential loss versus gain. But ultimately, the decision depended upon an assessment, based on limited information, that the hackers could be trusted to do what was wanted. Decisions, it appears, are generally based on only a small fraction of available information.

Even where there happens to be plentiful information, most judgments are based upon remarkably little of available information. As a benchmark, behavioral scientist Francesco Varela found that humans use only 20% of the visual information available to them.[15] This estimate was based counting the neurons associated with sensory receptors of "the outside world."

Even if information is placed front and center, it may be ignored or overlooked. The "Invisible Gorilla Experiment" was a research project on selective attention which became a book published in 2010. In the experiment, viewers were asked to watch six people, three of whom were wearing white shirts and three were wearing black shirts. The viewers were asked to count how many times someone with a white shirt passed to another person wearing a white shirt. During the 25-second video, someone wearing a gorilla suit walked into their midst, thumped his chest, and walked off. Remarkably, more than half of viewers did not notice the gorilla.[16]

Some decisions are undoubtedly formed based upon other information in addition to Varela's 20% absorption of visuals, but in a world of compressed time frames and a focus on summaries, partial or incomplete information is clearly the norm. Many people do not even expect to get all the information they need.

What does this mean for sellers? It means that since buyers will use only part of the information they have available to make a buying decision, a seller, while offering a lot of information,

---

[15]D. Yaniv, "Trust the Process: A New Scientific Outlook of Psychodramatic Spontaneity Training," *Frontiers in Psychology*, November 14, 2018. Francisco Varela cited.
[16]Christopher Chabris and Daniel Simons in their *Invisible Gorilla Experiment*. See youtube.com/invisible gorilla for a rendition of this experiment.

remains cognizant that much of it will be ignored as the decision-maker relies on preexisting beliefs and heuristics to make a decision.[17] One implication is that, except for some commodities, changes in terms or the current price tag are missed and may not have the expected impact.

Ideally, if you are a seller, your company will know which of the various price elements customers are using as purchase criteria. Note that price is made up of many elements to price. Buyers may focus variously or in combination on such elements as initial ticket price, total package price, total cost of ownership, discount percentages, warranties and operational costs, quality, residual value, and ratios of productivity and price. For instance, in the legal research field, for many years, the customer focus did not include the purchase price of research topics. Buyers cared only about the *net* cost of research, which was determined by deducting the amount reimbursed by a client from the total cost (the "chargeback").

This behavior suggests pricing strategies. For instance, if you *do* know what price elements are key to consumers, you can reduce or hold price on key pricing elements and possibly compensate by raising other elements of price.

For instance, one leading oil company found that during a financial downturn, motorists changed oil less frequently, but migrated to better quality lubricants. Further, they used their lower grade oils as the price benchmark. So, this company raised the price of its lower grade oils and kept its premium synthetic price constant despite increased demand – knowing that the increase in demand was not driven by consumer reevaluation of the premium oil's benefits. In this way, the company rapidly migrated customers to more expensive oil.

This is the essence of trust. It may differ from your assumptions. For a business, the ability to know what customers use as a litmus, and the ability to know what buyers do not notice is key. *Lack* of this knowledge is why companies may find that building trust takes

---

[17]M. Connors and P. Hamilton, "A Cognitive Account of Belief: A Tentative Road Map," *Frontiers in Psychology*, 2014, 5: 1588, p. 1599.

great time and effort.[18] Sadly, most companies do not know what their different customer segments use as a reference.

Sometimes this insight can be gleaned through simply getting to know your customer. Generally, it is good to ask customers what they want – but in an insightful way. For instance: a top-five US bank was surprised to find out that their online customers were least interested in fraud guarantees on their accounts. It turned out that these customers were confident that their online transaction was safe. Consequently, they did not value that feature.

Generally, it is good to ask customers what they want – but in an insightful way. In surveys, online users *reported* liking the guarantee because it seemed like a free bonus. (Why not?) Statistical examination of their online usage and whether they availed themselves of added security and guarantees showed the truth: this segment did not value optional security features and it would not change their choice of bank. Similarly, another segment was found to abhor digital banking and wanted physical cash, tellers, and safety deposit boxes. One interviewee described this as a desire to "fly below the radar." This was contrary to survey, but having proven true in practice, the bank moved to better accommodate this particular segment.

Typically, a "map" can be drawn of your market and what customers know and care about as the basis for trust. Such a map is illustrated in Fig. 2.1. The trust target can be a hard one to hit because it's a little target in a bigger field of attention.

Notice how the area of potential buyer awareness is large – perhaps infinite. The critical facts to customer decision are relatively small. Further, the information chosen for decision-making can be surprising. For instance, a London investment house said it had refused to take part in an investment offering a past scam because the offering firm's representatives wore two-tone shoes – a fashion *faux pas* that was a signal of untrustworthiness.[19]

---

[18]*Detroit Free Press*, October 27, 2019, p. B1. Regarding cover-up of water contamination; also Morning Consult survey, Ibid.

[19]This makes sense, beyond fashion correctness. Fraud requires self-confidence and self-centeredness. Wearing abnormal (for this environment) shoes signals self-centeredness.

Picture of Trust

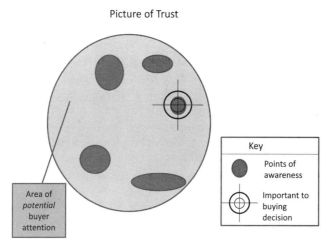

Fig. 2.1. Map of Buyer Trust.

Corporate managers, consumers, and CIA analysts rely upon history to develop a lens for determining the trustworthiness of potential interactions. This can work well, if they use the right criteria. For instance, financial reports, consumer ratings, and organizational assessments can be the basis for buyer decisions. Best of all are ongoing themes in building trust – hence messaging like Walmart's long-term use of the phrase "Always low prices."

However, the CIA has found a major pitfall if information is partial. This is that it is very difficult for people to change their criteria. Humans by nature are reluctant to change.[20] This can be overcome by the right teaming of management and periodic shifts in coverage. Companies do this well with their advertising agencies, but perhaps less well with those with product and pricing decision-making authority. Often, the management story of improved trust building in pricing is the story of the battle between truth and (self) deception, or the battle between complicated and simple.

[20]R. J. Heuer, Jr, Psychology of Intelligence Analysis, Center for the Study of Intelligence, Central Intelligence Agency, 1999, p. 9.

WELL, UNDERSTANDING THE BASIS FOR TRUST IS A LOT OF WORK

To manage trust, management needs to know the criteria which customers use to build trust. That can be very complex.

Consider the numbers. There are *at least* four dimensions to a commercial transaction:

- What is being offered?
- What are the buyer priorities?
- What terms (price structure and price level) frame the offer?
- What is the context for the sale?

For a typical market offer, there are many varieties of each component. For instance, for one residential telecom service, there are a dozen product/service choices – product, options, services, warranty, delivery, timing, bundles, upgrades, and so forth. There are many possible buyer priorities, including mission-critical, routine, agency, cost reduction. There are many price structures and many possible price levels. There are infinite contexts which can have a dramatic impact on price. As an example of context, the acceptable price of Coca Cola depends on whether it is on the beverage aisle, in a different part of the store, at a fountain or on a truck. In a different example, a leading college textbook publisher found that optimum textbook purchase price depended on such factors as the academic discipline and the tier of school.[21]

Context is an often-neglected factor, but in fact, it matters for everything in life. A study of hospital patients showed that the color of food plates affected how patients perceived the sweetness of strawberry ice cream served on those plates.[22] You must always consider context in building trust.

Thus, if a fair price is one which meets customer expectations, the offer must embody the right components: focus on one or a few

---

[21]R. Docters, *Contextual Pricing*, McGraw-Hill, 2012, p. 8.
[22]D. Oakley, "The Cook, the Fly, the Neuroscientist and the Food Lover," The MRC London Institute of Medical Sciences, December 20, 2016.

of the 12-plus components, address the right buyer priority (perhaps five choices/segments), and the right price structure, such as simple sale, rent/lease, guaranteed, "as is," turnkey, or DIY, for example.[23] Even more, it must reflect the right context in a world in which 12 or more contexts are not uncommon. This suggests that while there might be as many as 2,000 candidate prices to meet price expectations for an unremarkable product, only a few of those candidates might constitute the right way to gain trust through offer and price.

This is likely beyond most company's analytic capabilities. A sophisticated modeler or statistician might work with a dozen relevant inputs, with a less than 1% (12/2,000) chance of hitting the mark. Failure to do so makes trust unlikely.

Steps to Trust

How to build trust? There are some basic questions to help to ascertain whether you have trust now:

- Does the customer decide for themselves what is trustworthy? Often, companies have little influence on their customer thinking.

- Are you able to influence customer thinking? Be realistic! Few companies have the resources to transform distrust.[24]

- Use the right levers. This is where narrow versus broad applies.

If the customer decides trustworthiness for themselves, then your company is wasting limited resources to try and change it. So, you should observe customer behavior to see what they want.

If you cannot influence customers, accommodate their preferences. Don't lose credibility by making up unappealing arguments. For instance, General Motors Company found (again, having done so in 1980s) that gasoline efficiency mattered. Since some of their cars were not efficient, they promoted "range."[25] This meant bigger gas tanks. Gas guzzling engines remained the same. While this

---

[23]R. Docters "*Price is a 'Language' to Customers,*" *Journal of Business Strategy*, Vol. 24, issue 3, pp. 31–35.
[24]H. Gieskes, Lecture at Yale School of Management, November 2017.
[25]GM advertisements in the 1980s.

might have made engineering sense, it did not fly with buyers who still faced a big charge at the gasoline pump.

If you *can* influence your customers, then you should do so in order to better educate them as to what they need to know about your product or service – or to lift that burden from their shoulders. An upscale hair salon in New York City kept a sign in the window stating, "Trust us with your fashion."[26] They clearly made decisions for their clientele.

Unsure if you have this influence? Three means for assessing your influence on how customers view the offer:

- Look at the last negotiation. What did the other side want to focus on? Was your value argument accepted/ignored? Apart from price level, what was the focus? If your negotiator/ salesperson is adept at deflecting the customer focus on other issues, you still need to listen to the original customer inquiry – in most cases, they will come back to it.

- Offer payment choices. The choices may all result in the same net present value (profitability) to your company, but they may be quite different to the customer. For instance, one data package vendor offered two options. In one, an initial high purchase price came with a lower annual maintenance fee. The other had a lower initial price and a higher annual maintenance fee. The company was surprised that many buyers took the higher initial price/lower fee option.

- Split up the package of services over time. One major medical diagnostic imaging manufacturer found that its more cash-strapped customers would forgo a warranty for a lower price, even if that meant a higher total cost of ownership.[27]

Again, understanding trust plays a major role. So does shaping the offer. In the case of the diagnostic imaging equipment, the sales department complained that, for example, separating out the warranty for a CRT monitor would violate the trust of buyers. As it

[26]Aveda Salon, TimeWarner Center, New York, NY, September 23, 2019.
[27]Interviews with GE Medical Diagnostic equipment managers 2014.

turned out, this was because the same sales people had failed to point out the limited lifespan and vulnerabilities of the CRT, so less sophisticated buyers were chagrined at a failure. Given the sales force's omission, sales people liked a warranty which patched over the problem and avoided customer anger. With better training and documentation, there was no failure of trust, and better initial sales – and improved later replacement part sales as well.

In conclusion, trust is something which resides with the buyer. It is important to know what kind of trust they are willing to extend – narrow or broad? Creating trust through pricing or other tools available to management is difficult and requires consideration of many factors. One research tool you can trust is careful observation of the customer and his/her/their behavior.

Isolating the right trust factor requires the correct analysis. Generally, statistical observation is trustworthy, but only if broad enough to capture most of the possible drivers of customer behavior. Test many hundreds, not dozens, of relevant factors and then you will see what propels markets. It will also build customer trust as well as revenue success.

3

ETHICS AND ENTITLEMENT

Question: What are telltale signs of unethical situations?

If we act like prey, they will act like predators.
My Love Lies Bleeding by Alyxandra Harvey

What is the source of unethical behavior? Where does it come from? Are there telltale signs? Surveying the many instances of unethical behavior, it appears that a primary basis for this behavior is a feeling of entitlement, or justification, on the part of the unethical party.

That differs a bit from more traditional views that suggest wealth is a cornerstone of unethical behavior, or worse, a cornerstone, perhaps, of evil. A common identification with greed is "wealth"; those who command resources materially greater than do the rest of the population and therefore, are thought to be more prone to greed. And consequently, unethical behavior.

Christianity has intertwined wealth with discussions of ethics. The Bible makes note of the link between wealth and morals, or perhaps ethics. A relevant passage is Matthew 19:24:

> *Again I tell you, it is easier for a camel to go through the eye of a needle than for someone who is rich to enter the kingdom of God.*

A casual reading of this passage suggests that the rich are not entering heaven. A more literal reading merely suggests that wealth will be a severe impediment, hence the use of the word "easier" rather than an absolute "cannot."

We hypothesize that greedy and unethical behaviors are *more* associated with the perpetrator's *belief* that they can or should do something they know is greedy, than with exaggerated wealth. Greed results from someone's belief that they are either entitled or need (or are obligated) to be greedy. That "spark" of greed from a sense of entitlement can be instilled at birth or learned over time through circumstances. When resources are available without effort, there is little need for greedy behavior. When challenges occur, and a strategy to obtain resources is required, greed can be the motivating force of strategy.

WEALTH AND ENTITLEMENT

The distinction between wealth and entitlement can be subtle. The two phenomena coexist in a lot of cases. However, there are examples of the wealthy behaving in modest fashion and examples where the not-so-wealthy have behaved in an entitled fashion. We believe that this suggests that wealth is not the root of ethical problems. There are limits set by Noema XIX, which says "Tis better that one man be disabled from living voluptuously, than that another should live in want and calamity." This does not preclude ethical *behavior* by the wealthy. The language of Noema XIX is focused on an activity and a lifestyle, not a balance statement. Super-wealthy individuals who apparently live ethically include Warren Buffett, Azim Premji, and Bernie Marcus and Arthur Blank. These men generally have behaved well and have exhibited generosity and fairness, members of the Home Depot founding team, for example, reimbursed investors for an earlier start-up which lost money, even though he had no legal obligation to do so.[1]

---

[1] B. Marcus and A. Blank, *Built from Scratch*, Times Business/Random House, 1999.

There are a number of writers who have delved into the roots of ethical deviations. There are many commonalities. One writer has cited as elements:[2]

1. A feeling of omnipotence, or at least superiority.

   "To the omnipotent leader, rules and norms are meant for everybody but them. Crossing a line feels less like a transgression and more like what they are owed." This characteristic is related to Narcissism. One characteristic of narcissism is that it *"is a defense against rationality: you remake the scale so you are always at the center... It works, until you encounter someone who does not accept your gospel."*

2. Cultural numbness is when there is a need to integrate with a new culture (e.g., an employer), employees begin to speak the language, act according to norms, and dress to fit in. This prompts people to not consult their moral compass. If the company's moral direction is flawed, then ethical failure is likely to happen – especially if the company does not tolerate dissent.

3. Justified neglect is when people justify an unethical deviation because (often) it is small, and there is significant effort to correct the deviation. This is a slippery slope when you begin to rationalize actions and tell others.

The attraction of money, according to the German sociologist Georg Simmel, is the potential of what money *can* do.[3] This is why some unethical actors will undertake actions which by themselves do not mean wealth. An example is to seek power.

Power can have the same attraction as money. Machiavelli said a "prince" should not be inhibited by normal moral (or, we suspect, ethical) standards. At the same time, British philosopher Tim Dean has noted that morals are not fixed in black and white, but are

---

[2]M. Wedell-Wedellsborg, "The Psychology Behind Unethical Behavior," *Harvard Business Review*, April 12, 2019.
[3]A. Dao, "Money Talks," *The New Philosopher*, August–October 2018, p. 76.

simply the desire held by the stronger party – the individual who has the resources, and hence the power.[4] It's a vicious cycle.

Interestingly, a third form of resources emerged more recently. Harry and Meghan, the Duke and Duchess of Sussex, United Kingdom, stand to inherit property and about 20–30 million Euros, but their "brand" is estimated to be worth €200–500 million a year.[5] So, the relative values are (1) Brand, (2) Cash, and (3) Physical assets. Each may be converted to another under some circumstances, and so we might expect similar behavior for each type of asset.

So, when do people feel entitled to perform unethical, or greedy, acts? Examination of greedy and unethical actions suggests that there is a wide range of circumstances. The most obvious occurs when people face "resource dilemmas." Studies have shown that people make trade-offs to engage in behavior which is greedy, fair, or efficient.[6] So, when there is great need – for example, a need or desire for sustenance – greedy behavior increases. However, this behavior may be ameliorated or modified if participants perceive fairness as a consideration. Also, cooperation, if desirable, can further curtail greedy behavior.

These factors link to ethical principles. Noema XII lists justice as a principle. Justice must be balanced against the needs of ourselves and the needs of others. Therefore, great need has the potential of influencing material choices in ways which are not ethical. The actual balance is not calculable based on the Noema themselves.

Consider the use of untruths or lies. While lies are often a tool for achieving greedy goals, lies also often *follow* greedy actions. This is commonly seen in criminal cases. At the outset, lies are required for criminals to achieve their objective. Examples would

---

[4]T. Dean, "The Great Morality Scam," Ibid, p. 44.
[5]A. Philips, "Harry and Megan Became the Worlds Richest Personal Brand," *The Express*, October 14, 2021.
[6]"The Interplay Between Greed, Efficiency, and Fairness in Public Goods Dilemmas," *Social Justice Research*, September 2003, Vol. 16, Issue 4, pp. 195–215.

include entry into forbidden facilities or fraudulent agreements. However, most state laws recognize that more lies are needed to cover up the criminal act itself.[7]

Being the beneficiary of unfair actions, especially over a long period, leads to a thirst for more and strong resistance to counterclaims. For instance, some US states have long been net beneficiaries of federal taxes and funding. Alaska is a *net* beneficiary of federal expenditures (minus taxes) of $7,048 per resident. West Virginia comes in just above Alaska with subsidies of $7,283 per resident.[8] Yet, these two states are home to people who have some of the lowest confidence in the federal government and its programs.[9]

UNCLE SAM CAN BE UNETHICAL, ALSO

Sadly, the federal government itself sometimes will carry out unfair and unethical acts because it has the power to do. The government is not averse to acts of greed, for example, when its mission exceeds it budget or energy level. But more often, it relies upon its power. There are many examples, but most involve relatively weak groups. For instance, despite granting Native Americans sovereignty over their reservations, the prosecution of nonnatives for crimes such as murder against reservation inhabitants must be handled by state or federal criminal justice systems, not Native American justice systems. This is on top of hundreds of years of abuse and violations of agreements which still apply in the twenty-first century. In 1835, the Treaty of New Echota gave the Cherokees a nonvoting seat in the House of Representatives, but for nearly two centuries, Congress has not honored that promise. In November 2022, Chuck

---

[7]Lawinfo.com says that For you to be found guilty of being an accessory after the fact, you must meet the following criteria: You knew the person committed, was charged with or was convicted of, a felony, and you destroyed evidence, hid, helped, or lied to police and/or prosecutors for that person. Details vary by jurisdiction, but most recognize (and punish) falsehoods after the fact.

[8]WorldPopulationReview.com/state-rankings/federal-aid-by-state, 2022.

[9]Taking votes for J. Biden and D. Trump as a proxy for support for Federal government, the votes are quite decisive: Alaska: Trump 52.8%/Biden 42.8%, and West Virginia Trump 68.6%/Biden 29.7%.

Hoskin Jr., the principal chief of the Cherokee Nation, declared, "It's time to insist the United States keep its word."[10] This refusal to honor the treaty is a clear violation of ethics (Noema II and XX and XXIII), and it reflects poorly on our Congress.

Another example of unethical use of government power involves Iva Toguri, an American citizen born of Japanese parents. She was visiting Japan to aid a sick aunt when the Japanese attacked Pearl Harbor. Because she could not return home, and she could not obtain aid from her parents (who were forced into detainment camps), she took a job as a typist with Radio Tokyo (NHK). She then became an announcer on a program that included Allied prisoners of war reading news and sending messages home. The messages were frequently enhanced with commentary from announcers that the Allies should surrender. Toguri, as the announcer, was – as were as many as 20 other similar announcers – labeled "Tokyo Rose."

After the war ended, Toguri gave an interview in which she was described as "Tokyo Rose." That led to an investigation by military authorities who detained her for a year, but released her after concluding she had not engaged in treasonous activities.

When Toguri applied to return to the United States, journalist Walter Winchell began airing reports that she should be charged with treason. President Harry Truman bowed to political pressure and Toguri was arrested, tried, and convicted on one count of treason.

Two decades later, the two prosecution witnesses admitted that their testimony was false and coerced by the government. Truman violated Noema V by choosing the evil of coercing witnesses and engaging in "worldly contrivances." (Noema VI). In 1977, President Gerald Ford pardoned Toguri.[11]

---

[10]S. Romero, "Cherokees Asking U.S. to Honor 1835 Pledge for House Delegate," *The New York Times*, November 4, 2022, p. 1.
[11]https://en.wikipedia.org/wiki/Tokyo_Rose.

WOMEN AS VICTIMS

Women have for a long time been victims of those who feel entitled. There are examples galore. Among the more egregious was "Droit du Seigneur," a medieval European "right" which allowed nobles and rulers in Europe, Asia, and Africa to sexually use young women before their marriages. Even in the twenty-first century, this may still be happening in areas of Africa. Powerful leaders such as former Congolese dictator Mobutu Sese Seko were said to be offered young virgins by tribal heads when he visited their villages.[12]

More modern-day examples emerged in the United States in 2006 with the #MeToo movement as women began to recount how they were sexually assaulted by powerful men, such as Hollywood movie mogul Harvey Weinstein.[13] One prosecutor, in describing Weinstein's actions, declared: "They feared that he could crush their careers if they reported what he had done to them." Obviously unethical.[14]

How to address this ongoing problem is not as easy as some think. Many seem to believe that beliefs power the process. If so, then empowering women will work well. Clearly, there are some environments where determination and smarts can establish equality. For instance, Nancy Pelosi is generally thought to have been a very effective leader. This was a setting which leveraged traditional female social skills.

On the other hand, it is not clear that some more warlike environments offer the same opportunities. While there is evidence that women can handle bombings and heavy artillery attacks better than men, they are typically smaller in size and have not grown up learning to fight in the same ways. It is also possible that many

---

[12]F. Drury, "Crumbling in the Jungle: Eerie dictator's palace where Muhammed Ali trained for fight of his life alongside African despot who insisted on right to deflower virgins," *The Daily*, Mail.com, June 7, 2016.
[13]C. Lampen, "All the Testimony from Harvey Weinstein's L.A. Trial," TheCut.com, November 2022.
[14]More, Noema 15.

women find the ethical license to be violent less convincing, based on with what they grew up.[15] Missing the license to be violent, and possibly lesser self-righteousness, may be a disadvantage. To throw a young woman into battle, when this attitude development was neglected, is quite unfair. It is also unethical because promoting "animal appetite" is evil.[16]

SELF-RIGHTEOUSNESS

The trail to self-righteousness seems to follow some common paths. One is to be born to power and wealth in a society where predatory behavior is expected of powerful nobles or rulers. Another is to rise to power not effortlessly and to build anger or resentment along the way. This is, at least partly, a function of the person's character.

To begin with a positive example of how failure did not taint the individual, there is the example of George Mallory, who may be the first person to summit Mt. Everest. George Mallory is a heartening example of someone who failed, but did not reject the fairness of the result. In 1922, Mallory attempted to surmount Mt. Everest. He did not make it. In 1924, he came back more determined to succeed, but he was gracious in allowing team members equipment and to precede him. He may have succeeded, but he and his climbing partner were killed on descent. They were last seen about 800 vertical feet from the summit. His body was discovered in 1999. There was evidence he did summit. Whether he reached the summit remained the subject of debate nearly a century later.[17] Mallory seems to have done the second attempt from a feeling of duty and so represented a particular form of Victorian nobility and ethicism. It's also clear that Mallory was not looking for further conquests. No scaling of ambitions. No greed. Just a life ambition.

---

[15]The rate of violent crimes in the United States has women committing only 12% of murders. *2020 Statistical Briefing Book*, OJJDP. One could, possibly, draw similar conclusions from the 1973 tennis match between Bobby Riggs and the top-ranked female player.
[16]Noema II.
[17]J. Hemmleb, L. Johnson, and E. Simonsono, *Ghosts of Everest*, Mountaineers Books, 1999. Sir Edmund Hillary was once asked if Mallory might have preceded him in summiting Everest. His answer was "He might have been the first to climb up, but I am the first to climb down."

Anger and its cousin, entitlement, emerge from particular patterns. The examples below illustrate the different pathways that can result.

The multifaceted figure of Richard Nixon shows how failure and frustration can sometimes corrode ethical self-discipline. Nixon worked hard and served honorably as a Lieutenant in the United States Navy during World War II. He ran for President in 1960 and knew that he had lost the popular vote by 0.17%, or 112,827 votes, but was confident that the Illinois vote had been wrongly reported and there were issues with other state counts. When asked if he would challenge the results, Nixon said that he did not want to undercut confidence in the voting process and so stepped away from a result he clearly wanted.[18]

After that, and a frustrating defeat in a 1962 race for governor of California, Nixon clearly became embittered. So, in his 1968 race for President, he misrepresented the American position to leaders of North Vietnam, promising to end the war, but without specifics. After he was elected, he authorized a massive bombing of North Vietnam. In 1974, he resigned after being exposed in the Watergate scandal. Nixon presents a very different portrait. The derivation is unclear – whether it was circumstances or personality.

There is some evidence that unethical behavior may exist from childhood. A British Government Whitepaper concluded: "The idea that anyone is incurably wicked is distasteful and hard to except. But experience shows that there are some who will not make friends with society ever."[19]

One study suggested that whether the end result was significant or inconsequential did not deter those motivated by a sense of entitlement. The study showed higher income individuals were more likely to cheat in experiments and more likely to violate

[18]See G. Wills, *Nixon Agonistes. The Crisis of the Self-made Man*, Mariner Books, 2002; J. Farrell, *Nixon. The Life*, Vintage, 2018.
[19]A wide range of studies exist on this point, many or most of them suggesting some people are born evil or unethical. For example, E. Staub, *Roots of Goodness and Resistance to Evil*, Oxford University Press, 2015; also a reference in Giles, *Cartoons*, Daily Express, December 12th, 1965, regarding British Government Whitepaper (Unable to obtain full text of Whitepaper).

driving laws and regulations.[20] The study was based on seven experiments including an online dice game in which participants could win a cash reward only if they falsely reported their scores. The better-educated who self-reported as "upper class" were significantly more likely to cheat. In another experiment in which participants were told that a jar of candy was for children, those who self-reported as wealthy took twice as much candy from the jar as individuals who were not wealthy.

The greedy decisions may be made casually. Examples include Martha Stewart, who came from a working-class family and – while clearly talented – cut corners in building profits. She served time in prison for stock conspiracy during 2004–2005 and probation afterward. Given that she was a billionaire whose company went public for $1.9B, and the amount of the fraud was under $200,000 suggests that the criminal action was trivial, and likely represented more habit than need.[21]

Clearly, these sorts of actions violated Noema VI, which says that treachery steals away the right to worldly advantage, Noema IV which guides us to "Justice," and Noema XIV, which asks that you do the same to others as you wish done to you.

The combination of the actions of a sample of the "upper class" and the relevant Noema provides a strong indictment of the wealthy for engaging in greedy activities.[22] But it does not explain why so many of the wealthy behave unethically – there is often no apparent need.

Why do the social and economic upper classes feel entitled? It has been suggested that if elements of society go for a long time without facing bad experiences, they become oblivious to potential bad consequences of actions.[23] A sense of entitlement may be why there was "rage" among the wealthy over a cap on bonuses after

---

[20]S. Perry, "US upper classes more likely to lie, cheat and think greed is good, study finds," *The Minn Post*, February 28th, 2012.
[21]"Stewart Convicted on All Charges", CNN Money, March 10, 2004. C. Hayes, L. Eaton, "the Martha Steward Verdict: The Overview; Stewart Found Guilty of Lying in Sale of Stock", *New York Times*, October, 2004.
[22]We are linking wealth with identification of an "upper class." Given the disparity of (e.g.,) education, this would appear to be a reasonable linkage.
[23]See J. Ganash, "Extremist Rises as Experience of Its Consequences Fades," *The Financial Times*, December 6, 2018, p. 11.

the government bailout of financial institutions in 2008.[24] They apparently did not connect the receipt of the government money with a *quid pro quo*.

If the wealthy angry saw the bonus, which slipped out of their grasp, as a loss, then some of the anger may be explained by behavioral economics. This study of people's behavior shows a number of asymmetries in their perceptions of money. One is that people mind the loss of money more than they are cheered by the gain of an identical amount of money.[25] While amounts may be symmetrical, they are not all viewed as fair, according to behavioral economists. This would partly explain the anger of the wealthy.

Like entitled classes of past years, the current rich have worked to endow their children. They recognize that the world may not accord their children the resources they themselves enjoyed. There are many examples of schemes to shelter inheritors from inheritance taxes.[26] One such scheme which was not only unethical but also deemed illegal involved parents making donations to sports programs at an array of prestigious schools, including Stanford University and Yale University, as a way to get their offspring admitted. This "back door" to admissions provided a path for parents to avoid multimillion dollar donations and for students to be admitted based on applications that falsely represented the skills of applicants. Apparently, as little as $70,000 enhanced the likelihood of entry.[27]

In this chapter, we have examined the hypothesis that greed is a function of expectations. This differs from classical perceptions that greed is its own driving force.[28] We believe that the practice of greed is contrary to Professor More's Noema. We also note that the expectations arise from different sources, including the influence of peer groups and the perception of the weaknesses of potential victims.

---

[24]Krugman, Ibid.

[25]D. Kahneman and A. Tversky, "Choices, Value, And Frames," Cambridge University Press, 2000, pp. 484–486.

[26]R. Docters, et al., *Winning the Profit Game*, McGraw-Hill, 2001, p. 154 (on mixed asset pools, chapter on monetization).

[27]The Economist, March 16th, 2019, p. 24.

[28]Balot, supra, p. 138, quoting Thucydides.

SECTION III

TECHNOLOGY AND ETHICS

4

ARTIFICIAL INTELLIGENCE (AI) AND ETHICS

Every Generation has its own fears and dangers.

Know your 'why?'

Nancy Pelosi

Fear of innovation is pervasive. There are many examples of innovations over time which struck fear in observers, but ultimately were not major threats. Consider the armed bicycle. Before World War I, people feared that combining a bicycle's mobility with a machine gun would prove deadly. However, bicycles were not up to the task – they could not withstand the vibration caused by the firing of the machine gun and they were vulnerable due to lack of armor.[1] Other feared innovations, such as steam-powered submarines[2] proved unfeasible also.

Information technology (IT) and artificial intelligence (AI) are best evaluated ethically based on *present* capabilities. This is reflected in Noema VIII which suggests we focus on "the character of the present." A further caveat in Noema XI is that a "present evil

---

[1]R. Robinson, "Armed and Armored Bicycles and motorbikes," www.Landships/info/landships/softskin_articles/armed_bikes, (no date). Cites the UK Museum of Transport.
[2]The British "K Class" submarine could move rapidly on the surface, but suffered catastrophic failures.

is to be tolerated, in order to avoid... the future evil... infinitely greater than the present." This neatly sets the boundaries of the ethical inquiry: focus on the present, and don't do things which make it "infinitely" worse.

SCALING AND ARTIFICIAL INTELLIGENCE

Some greedy actions are small. For instance, a company which shifts their customer interface from providing live agents to providing customers with online forms and formulaic Q & A is taking something away from what they may have initially promised. This change is not huge – shifting the burden of publication and data entry to the user saves companies between $1.20 and $3.50 per form. And society tends to forgive small grabs. The legal expression for small violations of trust might best be described as *de minimis non curat lex*, translated as the law does not concern itself with trifles. However, when scaled to millions of customers and forms, the monies are substantial. When taking away live agents from vital services, for instance, in the health-care industry, the consequences may be very serious for the digitally challenged. "Scaling" is often an agent of greed, and its impact, motivation and influence on behavior often is underestimated. "Scaling" is an underestimated basis for increased greed.

ARTIFICIAL INTELLIGENCE

As technology evolves, some fear that AI and improved data gathering have the potential to fuel a huge growth in greedy actions. There is precedent. As early as 2016, thousands of Facebook users were tricked, using AI, into installing malware that led to their account information being hijacked.[3] There is no doubt that AI helps criminals and the greedy to be more efficient and successful. In particular, machine learning helps criminals:

---

[3] "Beware! Criminals are using AI to steal your personal details." Data Flair, October 25, 2019.

- More efficiently segment prospects, just as it does for legitimate marketers.

- Crack passwords and other defenses against machines (like CAPTCHA).

- Personalize messages and phishing attempts so that potential victims are more trusting.

None of these actions are, per se, greedy or wrong – or any different from normal marketing functions.[4] However, they do help greedy actors achieve their goals. Significantly, AI makes small greedy actions easier and cheaper to carry out, and thus, more scalable. It may have the effect of making small individual thefts worthwhile to smarter criminals, so it is worth asking what is the net cost of cybercrimes?

What is the capacity for AI to support unethical behavior? Technology today can give the unethical an advantage in fraud, theft, political manipulation, and identity theft. One technologist has opined: "AI is far more dangerous than nukes."[5]

If so, that violates one of Isaac Asimov's three laws of robotics: "A robot may not injure a human being or, through inaction, allow a human being to come to harm."

But, in fact, it is not clear ethically or technologically that this is the case.

For one thing, AI and IT in general have their share of failures. The Center for Security and Emerging Technology at Georgetown University's Walsh School of Foreign Service has reported 1,200 cases of AI failure over just three years. In a 2021 report, the center noted that these failures range from unintended, accidental incidents to intentional acts of deception and damaging misuse. For instance, AI programs tasked with drawing images from little or no starting point have produced elaborate images of houses and landscapes that do not exist. These are called "hallucinations." Other failures include mistaken diagnoses of the work they are

---

[4] K. Karlson "8 Ways Intelligent Marketers Use Artificial Intelligence." Content Marketing Institute, August 13, 2017.
[5] E. Musk, Speech at the South by Southwest Conference, 2018. Also C. Metz "Moguls and Killer Robots," June 10, 2018, p. 1 Business section.

supposed to do.[6] On top of being mistaken, the many layers of algorithms make it difficult to identify and correct the AI mistakes.

Part of the problem lies in the mechanism used by AI – an unselective acceptance/openness to feedback (i.e., adapting coefficients in the algorithms). For instance, when Microsoft launched an experimental AI-based online chatbot which mimicked a 19-year-old American girl, it went wrong. As a result of tweets from Twitter users, the chatbot began to use racist and sexually charged responses. IBM's chatbot Watson also began using profanity after perusing the online *Urban Dictionary*.[7]

At the same time, users can be influenced by the game or bot with which they are interacting. Because the interface between the program and the display or activation of the real-world device is what makes the program useable (or culpable), evaluation of AI must include analysis of users – humans. The video shooter game "Doom," in which a human player is pitted against an agent controlled by the computer agent, shows that the agent was far more violent than users. The average count of kills was:

- Single Player Human kills: 12.6

- Single Player Agent kills: 27.6

Thus, players see that the computer agent not only can win but also excels at killing.[8] To some, this appears to promote the notion of killing.

Is this ethical?

Not insignificantly, the impact goes beyond the game itself. Players of the game are likely to become more violent in their personal lives. A study published in *Developmental Psychology* showed that exposure to television is a contributing factor in the development of aggression. Because video games based on realism contain violent scenes and identification with aggressive characters,

---

[6]E. Brynjofsson and A. McAfee "The business of artificial intelligence: what it can and cannot do for your organization." Harvard Business Review, July 2017, p.

[7]F. Candelon, R. Charme di Carlo and S. Mills, "Why AI Needs A Social License," www.BCG.com/publications, February 22, 2022.

[8]The AI program Deep Reinforcement Learning Network powers the Agent.

we believe there is a similar effect.[9] This has a serious potential for deleterious impact:

- The players, particularly the young adults, may become more aggressive. This may not necessarily harm them, but is likely to do so. Many perpetrators of violent crimes as well as their victims are injured or killed after engaging in verbal aggression or physical aggression. That makes injury a more likely outcome of playing these games.

- Parents, family, and social contacts experience the increased aggressiveness. Females in particular become more aggressive verbally.

- Developers and retailers all participate in creating this negative influence. The developers may have profit to show for it, but may also become more aggressive and in return experience violent customers. In essence, developers and distributors are enabling harm.

This seems highly analogous to manufacturing a gun, a cigarette, prescription drugs or alcohol, or any other "good" which, if misused, are harmful. To say that consumers want such games and that developers/distributors did not mean to create harm is to ignore societal conclusions regarding other goods. AI is expected to become very important – a $1.5 trillion market in 2030. We note that Professor More wrote that to unleash a force which is bad, reflects on the person who does so.

Centrally, Professor More says: "That unless a Man has within himself a sense of things in his nature, there is nothing to be done."[10] This is the case with AI. There is no core. All it can do is add layers of algorithms, and as long as the algorithm enhances the result, the program will accept it. In the case of non-AI programs, for example, there is a core to the logic, such as in the computer programming language COBOL. This means that when there is a

[9]L. R. Huesmann, J. Podolski and L. D. Eron, "Early Exposure to TV Violence Predicts Aggression in Adulthood," American Psychological Association, www.APA.org. 2008.
[10]More, Ibid, Chapter III, section VII.

glitch, programmers can find the faulty code. This may be impossible on an AI program.

Some observers have attributed consciousness to an AI program. Further, they have attributed emotions such as anger to programs. Yet hostile or unfavorable reactions are not the essence of a being. Clouds in the sky also can appear angry and be violent, but they have no consciousness or awareness that anyone has ever detected. Complexity is not the same as consciousness.

REGULATION?

As you might expect, the unethical have welcomed AI into their tool kit. If AI and certain IT tools can assist the unethical, should the tools be curtailed or regulated? A number of bodies have called for regulation, including the British government.[11] The Henderson Institute, the think tank of the Boston Consulting Group (BCG), has suggested that companies become attuned to the roles that society sees as legitimate for AI and to adhere to those standards. They call this a "social license," a supplement to regulatory permission.[12] Would this regulation and social licensing make AI use more ethical?

Regulation is probably not the answer. It certainly is not the ethical answer. As noted by several observers,[13] AI is generally targeted to perform tasks currently performed by humans, especially unpleasant tasks. Further, the venue for this robotic service is shifting from the factory to settings such as social work and health care, cars, games, and advertising.[14] In other words, AI is taking on responsibilities. That is how AI differs from other tools, such as hammers, trucks, or calculators.

In the eyes of Professor More, AI falls short in several areas. AI has no sense of itself or its "nature." As a result, it cannot have a

---

[11]N. Dorries, Secretary of State for Digital, Culture, Media and Sport, "Establishing a Pro-Innovative Approach to Regulating AI," Report to Parliament, January 18, 2022.
[12]BCG, Ibid.
[13]"The Rise of Robots," *The Economist*, February 26, 2022, p. 16.
[14]H. Armstrong, "Machines that learn in the Wild," www.NESTA.org.uk, 2015.

sense of good or justice, nor can it be grateful. Finally, it does not produce laughter.[15] Without these attributes, such a thing establishes itself as "brute." While laughter may seem a secondary characteristic, it has prevented evil and serves as a good litmus test. Given that, if all we have is a dangerous device, we should treat it accordingly, just as we regulate or proscribe other unusually dangerous devices such as cannons and bombs.

This chapter reviewed the capabilities and ethical character of information technology and AI. That review was in the mixed world of AI and physical reality. What are the ethics of a totally virtual/digital world? The next chapter addresses artificial reality (A/R) and augmented reality.

---

[15]More, Ibid, Chapter III Section VII; Chapter XI Section II.

5

ETHICS FOR VIRTUAL WORLDS

Question: If it does not exist, can it be unethical?

> I do think that a significant portion of the population of developed countries, and eventually all countries, will have AR experiences every day, almost like eating three meals a day. It will become that much a part of you.
>
> —Tim Cook, Apple CEO

Increasingly, digital renditions of the physical world are drawing attention. There are online video platforms which can be completely digital such a "Second Life" or a mixture of digital and augmented reality (AR), such as "Horizon Worlds."[1] In these worlds, there are identifiable personae, representing you, who operate in a simulated environment and interact with other personae. A similar set of interactions occurs, though less visually, on social media applications such as Twitter and Facebook.

A key development on these immersive sites, from an ethical point of view, is the often ugly behavior of participants. For instance, Horizon Worlds has a "Murder Village," where virtual homicides are encouraged. There is also a broad tolerance of sexual

---

[1]Part of the so-called "Metaverse." There are currently over 50 such immersive sites, differing in scope, focus, and technology. See Compare Business Software/Horizon Worlds.com.

assault, and many participants indulge in these and other abusive behaviors.[2]

From an investor point of view, there has not been an overwhelming interest in the sites and the attendant violence. So far. There is growing sentiment that some of the violence occurring on these immersive sites is a reflection of an increasing anger and mental instability in the United States.[3] At the same time, larger companies such as Meta/Facebook are working hard to increase involvement and visitor counts.

What are the ethical standards for a virtual world? At first blush, it would seem like a consequence-free environment where there are no actual actions, and so a utilitarian such as Professor More should find little to condemn. However, Professor More is on sabbatical right now, but we have found a substitute fount of ethical rules who will offer comment: Immanuel Kant. We will use Kant's writings in *A Critique of Practical Reason* to consider the ethics of such a world.[4]

AMBIGUOUS BORDERS – FASHION AND PORNOGRAPHY

The dividing line between physical and intangible events is more ambiguous than one might imagine. Some might use the word fluid, but it's not the changes which matter. Rather, it's the nature of the two categories. Two examples will illustrate:

In 1966, a number of women were unhappy because some universities, businesses, and other institutions forbade them from wearing miniskirts, then one of the hottest fashion trends. Under the banner of the (probably facetious) *British Society for the Protection of Mini Skirts*, a group of women staged a protest outside the House of Dior on High Street London after Dior failed to include miniskirts in its fashion show. The protesters felt that the

---

[2]H. Lamb, "What can the Metaverse learn from Second Life."
[3]R. Aviv, M. Daum and M. Smith, "It's Not Just You. America's mental health crisis." *New York Times*, October 16, 2022, Sunday Opinion p. 1.
[4]Yes, some humor here. Prof. More died in 1687. Immanuel has not been seen since 1804.

skirt was a symbol of feminism and freedom and wanted to impart that message.[5] Symbols are, of course, intrinsically intangible – albeit powerful.

The debate over image versus physical reality is more heated and lasting when it comes to discussions of pornography and obscene behavior. One leading constitutional scholar wrote "that hard-core pornography is not an argument for sex – it is sex."[6] He specified that if a communication is only sex, with no societal/political messages, then the communication can be legitimately suppressed. Pornography in a virtual reality (VR) website can also be subject to being outlawed because it is a behavior which governments frequently ban.

Ethics, which extends beyond the scope of law,[7] also proscribes such behaviors, even if they are virtual. Although nothing physical is going on in a virtual world, can mental harm occur?

The answer, we believe, is yes; there is harm. The harm is most apparent when emanating from violence in the virtual world. If viewers are harmed through watching television, surely they are similarly influenced by being engulfed in a violent digital world. As previously described, the harm expands to other parties.

What about the acts themselves? Would destroying a virtual house or killing someone virtually violate ethics? Yes. This violates Kant's rule that imperatives which spring from internal sources should not be subordinate to other parties or influences ("a world beyond the senses").[8] Indeed, violence is corrosive and deadly in relationships among people – an understatement for sure.[9]

So ethically, participants in virtual worlds should be held accountable to their virtual actions. Remember: we are not talking legally, just ethically. This, in turn, suggests that architects and enablers of the virtual world should also be held accountable. This

---

[5]V. Ramos, Madam Blue Magazine, https://themadameblue.com/blog/the-history-behind-the-iconic-miniskirt-protest/, Spring 2022.
[6]F. Shauer, "Response: Pornography and the First Amendment," *University of Pittsburgh Law Review*, vol 40:605, p. 606.
[7]Ibid, p. 534. This refers to morality, not ethics but drives in the same direction.
[8]I. Kant, Foundations of the Metaphysics of Morals, as quoted G. Fletcher, Law and Morality" A Kantian perspective, Columbia Law Review 533, p. 408 (1987).
[9]Ibid.

includes Facebook founder Mark Zuckerberg whose Metaverse is a world which contains violent rhetoric and incitements to commit violence. It, therefore, has ethical consequences. Metaverse is Zuckerberg's attempt to extend his power and his wealth. He does not say that publicly, however.

THE ANTIDOTE TO VIRTUAL REALITY

We should not overlook the possibility that a virtual world is a damaging one for all participants. Compared to the real world, a forest in a digital world has very low content. After spending time in these digital worlds, some participants exhibit high levels of tension and irritability. Conversely, walking in a real world forest is a calming experience. A Japanese study found that spending time in nature can "improve your mind, optimize your health, and calm your spirit."[10] The study found that exposure to the varied plant life in nature helped to reduce negative thoughts and lowered activity in a part of the brain which is also active in those with manic depression. Another study of a practice called "forest bathing" reported that feelings of hostility in participants were significantly decreased.[11]

Based on these findings, the ethical implications are quite clear. Nature is good for people. According to Professor More "The Soul [is] taught how to effect and admire Creation and Beneficence which is dispersed through the whole Mass."[12] Professor More also says, "Nature were far diviner than Men."[13] Finally, more generally, Noema I says that the "acceptable, pleasant and agreeable" is

---

[10]K. Eriksson, "Hug a Tree, Fix Your Brain," Betterhumans.pub, April 28, 2020. This applies cross-species also. The Monks of New Skete report that puppies require a variety of new experiences. Being indoors does not provide the required enrichment. The Monks of New Skete, *The Art of Raising a Puppy*, Little, Brown and Company, 2011, p. 65.

[11]E. Morita, S. Fukada, J. Nagano, N. Hamajima, H. Yamamoto, Y. Iwai, N. Nakashima, H. Ohira, and S. Shirakawa, "Psychological effects of forest environments on healthy adults: Shinrin-yoku (forest-air bathing, walking) as a possible method of stress reduction" PubMed.gov, *Public Health* 2007 January 121(1):5463. Epub 2006 October 20.

[12]Ibid, Chapter IX, Section XV.

[13]Ibid, Chapter X, Section VII.

ethical. Noema V says that "evil must be shunned." We agree. If VR causes harm and bad behavior, it must be shunned.

However, there are forms of augmented reality which do not result in evil. These are less entertaining, but serve useful purposes. For instance, "Proximie" is a VR training tool for clinicians which allows them to share skills and best practices in a virtual operating room. Other VR tools such as "Hoppin' World" help create digital trade exhibitions, cutting travel expenses and waste. Other tools such as "Foretell Reality" are used for therapy or other specialized purposes. It is important to distinguish the mostly damaging from the useful and good.

One particularly troublesome area is the combined challenge of VR and AI. The threat here is that facial recognition means a program can observe human reactions and that AI can tailor the program's images to have the greatest impact upon the users. If an image looks, speaks, and emotes like a trusted person, there is a high probability of the VR being able to influence you.[14] Also, that package of presentation, deep profiling, and virtual presence may well be able to hijack your influence and authority.[15]

While that may seem daunting, do not forget that a similar result can result from the humble medium of paper. For many years, people have forged important documents and writing has dramatically influenced people.[16]

Upon reflection, it appears that the virtual world is not precluded from conventional ethical considerations. VR is populated with characters with a range of ethics, some good, some bad. So far, there has been little broad public categorization of sites as either good or bad. It would be a worthwhile ethical activity to do so. A task for another day?

---

[14]See video of robot "Sophia" on YouTube https://www.youtube.com/watch?v=S5t6K9iwcdw

[15]K. Shen and M. Khalifa, "Design for Social Presence in Online Communities: A Multidimensional Approach, *Transactions on Human-Computer Interaction*, June 2009.

[16]A list of influential books seems unnecessary, but would include *The Sorrows of Young Werther*, *Silent Spring*, and *On the Origin of Species*.

SECTION IV

SOCIETY AND GREED

6

INTANGIBLES, PIRACY, AND SHAPESHIFTERS

Question: How do changes in society's activities impact ethical standards?

A King takes half, a tyrant takes all.

Erasmus

So far, we have shown how some institutions and individuals use unethical behaviors to extract money, goods, and value from the rest of us. Also, we looked into why people cannot easily recognize those behaviors and so fall victim to the behaviors. Does this knowledge mean that more security and less disappointment is required?

Yes, but our discussion is not complete.

ETHICAL CONTEXT

The third dimension (in addition to Greedy Tactics + Susceptible Victim) is the nature of the coveted goods. There are big differences in ethical strategy in different property categories – in particular among tangible goods, intangible goods, and the shapeshifters[1] which inhabit both realms.

---

[1]Thank you J. K. Rowling, for familiarizing me with the term.

This is important because you need to adjust your ethical strategies depending on the context. This is not a call for cultural relativism, but rather recognition that the argument must be relevant to the topic. It's worth carefully exploring the "scope" or subject domain of ethical imperatives.

Some examples of treating intangibles differently from tangibles are found in the entertainment industry. Over the past decade and a half, the music industry, fighting against what it calls "piracy," invoked ethics to dissuade various (usually younger) listeners from duplicating music without paying royalties.[2] The industry has at times characterized such behavior as "theft."

Bach, Mozart, and other authors of valuable music, however, would not call it theft. In accordance with Socratic beliefs, they believed that music and writing did not stem from the author or composer – it stemmed from God.[3] Hence, it was a common practice among composers to "borrow" elements of other composer's compositions. There is current generational support for that view. Some 38% of survey respondents 16–24 years of age say they have "illegally" copied music, and 24- to 44-year-olds are not far behind.[4] There is far less support from those over 44 years of age.

Why are Mozart, Bach, and 16- to 44-year-olds opposed to the views of middle-aged music and entertainment executives? The reason may be greed and the big differences between tangibles and intangibles. Intangibles differ from tangibles economically, emotionally, operationally, and in understanding. These differences include the relatively low incremental costs for sharing and duplication. In the classic "public goods" case of radio, it costs no one anything for content to be shared with another (incremental) listener. For this reason, most broadcasting and point to multipoint distribution arrangements do not try to limit listeners/viewers. In

---

[2]Associated Press "Teen convicted of illegal Net downloads," March 7, 2005. The music industry is apparently concerned about its image, and so has refrained from earlier comments condemning the action in moral terms.
[3]Phaedo.
[4]F. Richter, "Music Piracy is Still Prevalent in the Age of Streaming," Statristica.com, April 8, 2022.

fact, in most countries, advertising revenues drive broadcasters to seek larger audiences.[5]

In contrast, where advertising and large growth of users are not available, sellers of intangibles, such as software and databases, charge per user or viewer and are convinced that offering the intangible for little or nothing would hurt revenues and profits. This is why AOL fought to keep users for $24.99 per month in the face of free alternatives, and for many years Microsoft strictly guarded its DOS, Windows, and Office products with passwords and other barriers.[6] Such an approach may not last forever and may not be optimal, but guarding the value of software can result in huge profits in the near term. The result has been the creation of high proportion of plutocrats in the software, media, and financial industries.[7]

MONEY

Money is a commodity which changes form from tangible to intangible, and sometimes back again. In the distant past, in a barter economy, money was always tangible, whether it was gold, silver, sheep, or stones, for example. Over time, however, the uses of money have become "productized." Therefore, loans, currency transfers, futures, and options are intangible. Money has moved from tangible (e.g., gold) to include bank accounts, transfers (e.g., Paypal, Zelle, etc.), and other services.

---

[5]For instance, management reports for Netflix all place a central role on viewership/listeners. For example, Value Line Investment Survey, "Netflix, Inc.," 2020, p. 2343.

[6]Companies often do try to build a wall around their products and then fret that they cannot easily lower prices or practice price discrimination to attract new users. Jean Manuel Izaret has pointed out that there are ways of overcoming these issues. In a low-incremental cost/high-initial cost product, the terms of the contract can be adjusted so that there is no need to amortize costs rapidly. Rather, contracts/purchases can be made for longer periods of time so lowering the initial burden of purchase.

[7]About 7 of the top 10 richest people. K. Dolan, C. Peterson-Withorn "World's Billionaires List. The Richest in 2022" Forbes.com, June 2022. Note that these sorts of lists typically miss very old money, e.g., the Grosvenor Family, which owns much of London.

A materialistic view is that both intangibles and tangibles can be "owned" and there is little difference. The Pythagoreans of the first century AD, however, suggest:

> ...*while everything assigned as private property by civil law shall be so held as prescribed by those same laws, everything else shall be regarded in the light indicated by the Greek proverb (ioprover) 'Among friends all things are held in common' (amicorum esse communia omnia)...[Therefore] bestow even upon a stranger [anything] which costs us nothing to give... Let anyone take fire from our fire.*[8]

These ancient ethical adages seem highly applicable to software and intellectual property. There is no loss in utility from copying and reusing software. In fact, often the utility is enhanced. For example, look to communication software. The complexity and variety of software makes it difficult for any new business-to-business (B2B) software to communicate with desired partners. Large software providers such as IBM therefore test beta versions with their best customers. This allows them to make the software broadly compatible and to take out patent protection.[9] If such beta trials were not possible, then commercially released software would often fail to serve the desired purposes.

So, it appears that IBM likes to hold some things in common with its friends, although they might be surprised to hear their rationale dates back to Roman times. The rationale for doing this has the same root purpose: to create and sustain a community. This is important, both to individuals and groups of people, whether it be small communities, businesses, or larger entities.[10]

---

[8]K. Eden, *Friends Hold All Things In Common*, Yale University Press, 2001, pp. 104–105. This superior book has a rich discussion of intangible versus tangible goods and how people thought about that difference.
[9]Interview with software expert William Moran, August 2022.
[10]Interview with William L. Moran, Sr., former senior systems manager at IBM.

ETHICAL SHIFTS

Where is this going? Over the last quarter century, the knowledge, intangible, and intellectual property economy has risen inexorably.[11] Services and software have grown while tangible products have declined as a portion of the economy. It is likely that services and software offer benefits and cost-effectiveness superior to most tangibles in some applications, and so consumers embraced the intangibles because their lives were improved. Some examples of the transition include: computing centers transitioning to purchasing software as a service (SAAS), and computing done remotely (in the cloud.) This efficiency of cloud architectures shrinks goods ownership and service costs. There are many other examples of shifts such as listening to recorded music versus attending a live performance.

These shifts implicate ethics. In some cases, the nature of capture of value shifts dramatically, and with it, the ethics. For instance, in the case of automobile leasing, the value shifts from manufacturer to lessor, car owner, and driver. The lessor is able to purchase many vehicles and obtain excellent prices from the manufacturer; the lessor benefits from the tax differences between driver and owner, and the driver gets a good rate. The losers are the dealers who rely on vehicle sales and the tax authorities.

Similarly, with electric vehicles (EVs), there is the benefit to buyers which comes at the expense of the government, other types of cars and possibly the environment.[12] EVs do not pay highway taxes, as they do not buy gasoline. EVs have benefited from targeted tax breaks from Congress and localities. It is also not clear whether owners will pay for higher disposal/recycling of metals from the car. Further, the source of pollution shifts from the EV, which is emission-free, to the local power plant which provides the electricity. If

---

[11]J. Bush and M. Chu, "Forward Thinking on the Transformative Role of Intangible Assets in Companies and Economies with Sian Westlake and Jonathan Haskel," McKinsey Global Institute, January 12, 2022.
[12]A. Georgiou, "How much better are electric cars for the environment?" Newsweek.com, June 4, 2022. The article notes that EVs are probably worse for the environment in the US Great Planes, Midwest, and the South. They may be worse than hybrids everywhere, and these studies do not reflect differences from batteries and car lifespan.

that plant uses coal or a low-grade bunker, total pollution rises.[13] Nonetheless, Tesla and other EV manufacturers reap credits and revenues. This squarely violates Noema XV,[14] which says "you must do the same to another… without causing injury to any third party."

Within service categories, there is a rapid shift from personal services to automated or digital. Examples include communications, where communication in person has shifted to online digital (e.g., Zoom); in security, where monitoring has shifted from people to computer scans, and in medicine where digital testing has partly replaced in-person examination.

ETHICAL EVALUATION

The damage to community from the digital shift is clear. It begins with school children who were taught remotely during the pandemic, resulting in impaired learning and social development.[15] Company morale suffered. Peggy Noonan wrote an opinion piece in the *Wall Street Journal* which highlighted the problems of remote work such as isolation and stiff hierarchy as well as the end of mentoring, learning about colleagues' works and experiences.[16] A Zoom screen is no substitute, Noonan declared. These many abstractions destroy community and the learning which comes from physical proximity in work.[17]

The utilitarian ethical question posed by this evolution: "Is this change good for most people?" Often such changes represent a net good for society. Studies have shown that, thanks to software, we enjoy enhanced logistical planning, which renders ships and vehicles more efficient. Oil consumption is less critical today than

---

[13]In addition, EVs are likely to promote more mining of the deep sea floor, with consequent destruction of the environment.
[14]Refer to Chapter 9.
[15]J. Anderson, "Harvard EdCast: The Negative Effects of Remote Learning on Children's Wellbeing," February 18, 2022.
[16]P. Noonan, "The Lonely Office Is Bad for America," *The Wall Street Journal*, July 30, 2022, p. A16; "Nothing to lose but their laptops," *The Economist*, January 19, 2019, p. 80.
[17]Based on work at McKinsey, Booz Allen, and BCG, it's clear that most companies are not equipped to accurately calculate these costs.

during the oil crisis of the 1970s. For instance, avoiding bottlenecks and the reduction of partially filled trucks and increase in full trucks is substantial.[18]

In some cases, there is a net cost to the change for society. There is some argument that ride-sharing drivers lose money while their employers, such as Uber and Lyft, were profitable. But we can believe that improved efficiency and volumes are a net positive to society and so are ethical.[19]

ETHICAL RIGHTS

As tangibles and intangibles have changed over time, so has the drive to own and control intangibles. If intangibles are held in common, and not easily converted to valuable tangibles, they are treated less possessively, recalling the common practice of renaissance composers to "borrow" elements of other composer's compositions.[20] No so, today. Between 3,000 and 5,000 copyright infringement suits are filed annually.[21]

Outside the area of music, companies such as IBM view patent licensing as a major source of revenues, generating $27 billion from 1996 to 2010.[22] All this is evidence that regardless of the sector, intangibles are growing in importance and value. The implication, as articulated by several McKinsey & Company authors, is that "Executives – and governments – searching for sources of growth should arguably pay more attention to the full range of intangible

---

[18]On efficiency improvements, see "AI is Changing the Logistics Sector," *International Finance*, March 21, 2022.
[19]Noema VIII.
[20]"Musicologist says Mozart, Bach 'borrowed.'" *UPI Archives*, May 31, 1985.
[21]Transactional Records Access Clearinghouse (TRAC) at Syracuse University, September 29, 2017.
[22]"IBM's DROP IN DIRECT IP LICENSING MAY BE A REFLECTION OF SECULAR CHANGES IN TECH, LAW, *IP Close Up*, May 4, 2021. (Article does note two-year drop over 2020–2021).

assets."[23] This is consistent with economic observation of current practice under current law.

BUT IS IT GOOD AND ETHICAL?

The important adjunct to the discussion of tangible and intangible is the difference to society and the impact on wealth. One difference between current plutocrats and previous generations is that their control of intangibles is explosively more profitable. This means that some will grow wealthy beyond common experience. This creates rifts in community, which then suffers.

Community that includes different groups of people (and animal species) has been credited with many benefits, including a better chance of survival.[24] Some argue that community is evolutionary and a benefit.[25]

Vesting one person, or a small group of people, with disproportionate wealth destroys community. Very few people are able to mix with billionaires. That exclusion is mutual: billionaires guard access.[26] Even moderate levels of wealth can be exclusionary. This matters because, as Professor More notes, isolation can turn people into "gods or beasts."[27]

The opposite side of the tangible/intangible evolution is that intangibles, such as digital, have provided access to previously limited or unique physical events. The distribution of the music of the Beatles, Bee Gees, and Beyoncé, as well as sports events and education via online, has to be beneficial to everyone.

---

[23]E. Hazen, S. Smit, J. Woetzal, B. Cvetanovski, M. Krishnan, B. Greg, J. Perrey and K. Hjartar "Getting tangible about intangibles: The future of growth and productivity?" McKinsey & Company, June 16, 2021 Discussion Paper, p. 18.
[24]D. Marques, Happiness.com, August 2022. Benefits of community are reported as (1) Support and safety (2) Connection and belonging (3) Influence (4) Sharing · (5) Learning (6) Acceptance (7) Many connections and opportunities.
[25]B. Grinde, "An Evolutionary Perspective on the Importance of Community Relations for Quality of Life" Open Access Volume 8, Article 828279.
[26]Of the four billionaires I have met personally, access to three was closely guarded. In one case via reinforced walls and armed guards. One billionaire had no obvious defenses at hand.
[27]More, Epistle to Readers, Chapter VI, Section XVI.

The shift of wealth to the intangible means that we need to be vigilant as to how technology evolves.[28] Whether a society can be vigilant for long, however, is doubtful. President Dwight D. Eisenhower in his 1961 farewell address to the nation warned the United States to be vigilant against the growth of the military industrial complex. It would appear that warning did little to deter that growth and its accompanying problems.

If intangibles represent a different ethical category to tangibles, it would make sense for virtual reality to pose its own set of ethical challenges.

---

[28]The famous robber Willy Sutton was asked: "Why do you rob banks?" His answer supposedly was "Because that is where the money is."

7

ETHICS, HUMANS, AND LOBSTERS

Question: Should you care about remote evil?

Truth is Independent of its Roots.

William James

Every year about nine million innocents are boiled alive. The experience has been proven to be agonizing: creatures with exoskeletons feel heat more than any other kind of animal, according to various university studies, such as Queen's University in Belfast, Ireland.[1] The practice of boiling lobsters alive may offer some confidence of safe food, but it is unnecessary. Killing them immediately before dropping them in a pot of boiling water also works. When boiled alive, lobsters release cortisol, the same hormone that humans release during times of fear or stress. Cortisol increases sugar (glucose) in the blood system, which may have a negative impact on a diner.

Of course, we used to boil people alive, although not recently, and at least not generally. In the mid-1500s, for instance, thieves were boiled alive in Hyde Park, London. More recently, Shining

---

[1] "Study Says Lobsters Feel Pain," NPR, November 16, 2007; B. Sharkey, "Switzerland Bans Boiling Live Lobsters, Calling it Animal Cruelty," Simplemost.com, September 16, 2018.

Path terrorists in Peru have been reported to have boiled some of their victims to death, and the militant Islamic group ISIS has been said to have killed some prisoners by immersing them in boiling engine oil.[2] The sight was said to be as horrendous as it sounds.

So what are the ethics of inflicting such a cruel death on people or animals? For Professor More, the answer is simple. Such unpleasantness "is the worst of evils."[3] That part is quite obvious. A more difficult question is what are the ethics merely *observing* such cruelty? Can you ethically ignore the unspeakable?

This where the rules are ambiguous. The Noemata suggest that you have an ethical obligation to seek justice, and that sights such as a boiling death are "evil."[4] Importantly, this sort of thing is (fortunately) rare, but clearly there is no need for it. Many civilizations have survived and prospered without boiling people alive.

So why are millions of lobsters boiled alive? Mostly it's because it's not controversial because of the convenient myth that they feel no pain. But this is not so. A 2007 study at Queen's University, Belfast, Ireland, showed that lobsters dropped in boiling water experience extreme pain for 2–3 minutes.[5] Despite there being several ways to humanely kill lobsters before placing them in boiling water or steam, it is the predominant means of preparation. The ultimate responsibility lies in the entire chain of supply – from lobstermen to distributors to the cooks who drop them into the boiling pots. If this sounds similar to the pipeline for human trafficking and modern sexual slavery, it is quite analogous.

Many people don't want to hear this. In part, we suspect this is because lobsters, while intelligent social animals, are viewed as things, not a sentient beings. But if a lobster is an entity not deserving of consideration, what about beagle puppies? In fact,

---

[2]Death by Boiling, Wikipedia; *Shining Path. InSight Crime*, March 27, 2017.
[3]Noema I and Noema XV. There is also religious support to more humane killing of animals. In Bali, the Hindu priests declared that the practice of cutting up turtles while they were alive was contrary to the religion. A. Paddock, "On Bali's Beaches Saving a Species from Becoming Dinner," *The New York Times*, July 8, 2018.
[4]Noema II, "what is... unpleasant or any ways incongruous to... Life and Perception is evil. And it if finally tends to the destruction of being, it is the worst of evils."
[5]Prof R. Elwood, Queen's University, *Journal of Animal Behavior*, repeated in part on NPR, November 16, 2007.

beagles are used for animal testing more commonly than most people are aware. These animals clearly feel pain. They suffer when abused. In 2022, federal agents rescued 4,000 beagle puppies from Envigo, a breeding and research facility in Cumberland, Virginia. The beagles were "hungry, sick, mistreated and, in some cases, dead."[6] There seems to be little doubt about their intended fate.

The ethical principles laid down by Professor More clearly balance the welfare of different parties and forbid injury to third parties. The pertinent Noema, which we have quoted before, says we must "...look to the duty toward others... whatever good you wish to be done to you in the given circumstances, you must do the same to another... without causing injury to any third party."[7] Those who ignore this rule would turn a blind eye to deliberate harm to lobsters, puppies, and human slaves. This is unethical, whether it is a lobster, a beagle puppy, or a human being.

While Professor More writes about ethics as applied to humans, Kant has a much broader definition: "Humanity covers all rational beings... if someone asks whether an animal or a child... has rights he is asking whether the categorical imperative applies to it."[8] When lobsters, puppies, and human slaves are not accorded rights and freedom from deliberate harm, this, again, is unethical.

This chapter has described ethics as applied to some dire actions. While torture may seem, per se, unethical, it is widespread. As a practical matter, these ethical violations are easy to avoid in many cases. The continued existence of such violations suggests callous indifference or intention on the part of participants, including observers.

---

[6]A. Rubin and J. Jimenez, "An Outpouring of Help for 4,000 Floppy-Eared Survivors," *The New York Times*, July 20, 2022, p. A9.
[7]Noema XIV.
[8]R. Scruton, *Kant: A Very Short Introduction*, Oxford University Press, 2001, p. 86.

8

GENERATIONAL ETHICS

Question: Why do younger/older people not respect my ideas or contributions?

We have a saying in the movement
that we don't trust anybody over 30.

Jack Weinberg, leader of Free Speech Movement,
San Francisco Chronicle, 1964

It should surprise no one that the opportunities presented to different generations are not equal. Some generations had bright economic opportunities, some lived through a depression. Some generations faced a world at war, others fought a war in faraway places, not of their choosing, a few enjoyed peace. Some generations enjoyed a positive vision of society and its future, and others saw their prospects dim as they worked hard – and failed – to maintain their standard of living. Frequently, one generation blamed another generation for its misfortune.

What are the ethics of generational conflict? Professor More writes that one must look to your duty toward others. More specifically, to develop the "foundations of Sincerity, Justice, Gratitude, Mercy and Compassion."[1]

---

[1]More, *Ibid* Noema 12.

One difficulty in evaluating generational ethics is that the ethical standard and the opportunity and resources differ by generation. There may be a divergence on how to measure opportunity and wealth. For instance, a common baby-boomer position is that society should offer equality of *opportunity*.[2] A common Millennial/Generation X/Generation Z (henceforth "Millennials") position is that opportunity is secondary to whether equality has been actually *achieved*.[3] Results are what matter for those generations, it appears.

This chapter examines generations which exhibited or are exhibiting a lack of empathy and affection for each other: Baby Boomers (born between 1945 and to 1961), the Millennials (born between 1981 and 1996), and Generation Z (born in 1996 or later.) This distance is exhibited by the Gen Z chant "OK Boomer" and stickers saying "OK Boomer, have a terrible day."[4] This phrase, or message, is appearing on a broad swath of wearables and millions of tweets. Essentially, it is a snarky response to comments from basically any person over the age of 40 who is perceived as condescending or misunderstanding of the younger generation.

Is that fair? Difficult to say. One view is that teenagers are not wrong; they are "living at the fault lines of a culture."[5]

A BOOMER VIEW

Many of the Boomers do not view of younger generations very positively either. They see Millennials as being slaves to smartphone use (48%), having a sense of entitlement (41%), and exhibiting laziness (35%).[6] As the percentages show, this view of younger generations is not homogenous across the Boomer generation, but it is indicative.

---

[2]M. Friedman, Capitalism & Freedom, University of Chicago Press, 1962, p. 195.
[3]T. Lorenz, "OK Boomer Marks the End of Friendly Generational Relations," *The New York Times*, October 29, 2019.
[4]The age group 8–11 is generally considered more socially passive. M. Anthony, "The Social and Emotional Lives of 8–10 Year Olds," *Scholastic Parents*, November 8, 2022.
[5]J. Webster, "Your Mind and What is Around It. We Can't Divorce Our Physiological State from the Forces that Dictate Our Lives," *The New York Times*, October 16, 2020, p. 4A.
[6]"Study Reveals Relationship Between Baby Boomers and Millenials," Olivet Nazarene College, 2022.

Where there is inequity between the generations, the potential for anger is heightened. Never mind that inequality may be hard to define, but in the eyes of different generations, there is an ethical issue. The result is conflicts in organizational settings, such as the workplace. Boomers say that they are victims of age discrimination by Millennials.[7] Millennials say they are subject to condescension and lack of respect.[8] Both sides of a generational conflict want control and resources that are not (yet) theirs. There may also be a conflict in moral precepts, e.g., the primacy of factual certainty.

DIFFERENTIALS

What are the ethics of this generational divide? This question depends – in large measure – on what each side has received upon reaching maturity and what responsibility of each side has to the other.

According to Professor More's Noema XIX: "'Tis better that one man be disabled from living voluptuously, than that another should live in want and calamity." Could this be relevant to the complaints of the Millennials? An overwhelming number of Millennials say that life is harder now than it was for baby boomers at the same age.[9] For example, 40% of Millennials say that owning a home is impossible. This prompts questions. Is that a big difference? Are the Millennials right in their assessment of the differences between the two generations?

Let's say that the differential is material. Does that meet the standard of Noema XIX? Is not owning a home the same as "want and calamity?" Probably not.[10]

If the situation does not rise to action under Noema XIX, it may rise to Noema XXII which says: "'Tis good and just to give every man what is his due, as also the use and possession there..." So what is due to each generation? One source of insight is the comparison of wages vs. productivity. Noema XXII suggests they should move in parallel.

---

[7]T. Lorenz, "OK Boomer Marks the End of Friendly Generational Relations," *The New York Times*, October 29, 2019.
[8]Lorenz, Ibid, p. 5.
[9]T. Schmall, "A Lot of Millennials Think Owning a Home is Impossible," *The New York Post*, February 15, 2019. From https://nypost/201902/15.
[10]Full disclosure: the authors are baby boomers who own homes.

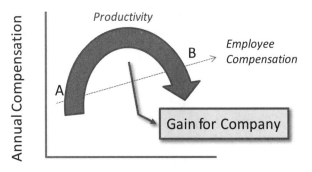

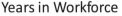

Years in Workforce

Fig. 8.1A. Lifetime Gain/Loss on Employees.

MILLENNIAL ECONOMICS

What is "due" to a worker may be measured in many ways. These include wages (hourly or other) that reflect tenure or skills or overall productivity. It may also reflect the success of the employer/ venture or the worker's needs. This can result in a disagreement on the best measure, but key to this question is that compensation tends to increase over the time employed.

Classical economics sees the relationship between compensation and productivity as diverging over a worklife.[11] This is illustrated in 8.1A. The productivity of workers is seen to start low, as they do not have experience, then rise to a high point as they learn and remain vigorous. And then, productivity declines with age, lower energy, and less endurance. Meanwhile, compensation (dotted line) tends to rise over time based on tenure and seniority (Fig. 8.1A).

Employers also notice that employee productivity becomes lower as workers approach retirement.[12] From the point of view of younger workers, there is unfairness. While at point A, they are paid less than their productivity, at point B, they may see that they earn more than their productivity, but they remember the years when it was less.

---

[11]G. Becker, *Human Capital*, University of Chicago Press, 3rd Edition, 1994.
[12]C. Rampell, "In a Hard Economy for All Ages, Older Isn't Better...
Brutal," *The New York Times*, February 2, 2013, p. B1.

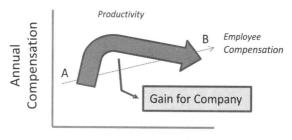

Fig. 8.1B. Lifetime Gain/Loss on Employees. Initial Productivity Advantage.

Many Millennials and younger generations say that they are particularly productive immediately because of their immediate grasp and affinity for digital tools. This means that they enter the workforce very productively, indeed, above traditional compensation levels. This is illustrated in Fig. 8.1B.

In Fig. 8.1B, the productivity of workers just a few years into the workforce is relatively high, perhaps because of education in software development. Yet, their wages are relatively low. Not accounting that entry wages have traditionally been low, and that there are many things one learns inside a company, you can see why Millennials feel unfairly treated. The period of investment by the company at point A is short or nil.

Even apart from productivity, there is some support for the feeling of unfairness by Millennials. Measure of actual hours worked seems like a simple measure of contribution to the enterprise. For the United States, the number of hours worked per year has trended upward from 2010 to 2021.

2010: 1772 hours

2021: 1791 hours[13]

At the same time, the opposite trend has occurred in other countries. Assuming the number of Millennials increased in the mix of

---

[13]OECD Statistics, 27 September, 2022, 06:52 UTC (GMT).

workers over this time, it appears that the younger US generations
work more hours.

BAD BOOMERS

Further, there is broad agreement that on-site work has become less
of a source of satisfaction.[14] One factor in this, say various top
managers, is that work has become less collegial and harder to
tolerate. So, the Millennials are working longer and enjoying it less
– another reason for them to be unhappy.[15]

Whose fault is this?

The Millennials point to the Boomers as the architects. This may
well be true. Many companies, for instance, cut research and
development (R&D) over the last two decades. This gave those
companies higher margins, but likely cut back on future productivity. A number of companies like GE and Kraft Heinz Company
cut future prospects until they collapsed so that when GE Chairman
and CEO Jack Welch retired in 2001, GE was worth only 20% of
its former value.[16,17] The Noema XXIII says "that a man may so
behave himself, as that what was his own by acquisition or donation, may of right cease to be his own."

By applying that Noema, the Boomer generation does not come
off well. Many excellent companies were damaged during Boomer
stewardship.[18] For example, two decades after Welch retired, he is
generally thought to have destroyed GE, although recognition of
that was slow to develop. He should be recognized for authorizing

---

[14]J. Albanese, Inc., "Why Employee Satisfaction is at an all-time Low",
October 24, 2018.
[15]"Nothing to lose but their laptops." *The Economist*, January 19, 2019, p. 80.
[16]J. Liu, US Workers are among the most stressed in the World, New Gallup
Poll Shows, June 15, 2021; L. Collins "Job unhappiness is at a staggering
all-time high, according to Gallup," August 12, 2022.A. Black, "Beleaguered
Kraft-Heinz Pays Price for its R&D Diet," *Wall Street Journal*, March 12,
2019, p. B1.
[17]H. Olen, "Jack Welches Toxic Legacy," March 2, 2020; see also A. Black
"Beleaguered KraftHeinz Pays for Its R&D Diet," *The Wall Street Journal*,
March 12, 2019, p. B1.
[18]Evidence of this is that occupancy of the Fortune 50 slots turned over 54%
in the period 1960–2005.

the growth of GE Credit, but he also destroyed the core businesses and shipped untold jobs overseas.

Noema XXIII applies to politicians as well. In particular, Boomers George W. Bush and Donald Trump were ranked among the 10 worst Presidents in a Siena College Research Institute poll in 2022. Out of 46, Bush was 35th and Trump was 43rd. Greed played a major role in the motivations of these two Presidents. In an interview with *New York Times* reporter Maggie Haberman, Trump said his ambition in running for office was to be "more famous."[19] In 1994. Bush told a reporter who asked why he pushed so hard for Roger Horchow, a retail catalog magnate turned Broadway producer, to be chairman of the National Endowment of the Arts, Bush replied, "He gave money to my father."[20] In 2022, another politician from the Boomer generation, Vladimir Putin, invaded Ukraine, unleashing untold deaths and destruction.

Sometimes it is difficult to blame another generation for what can be fairly classified as bad luck. By 2022, a disaster awaited Millennials in the housing market. For many, houses were too expensive. But those who had bought will begin to see a housing bust in the next few years, as Boomers begin to sell to downsize or move into retirement communities.[21] This will cause prices to fall, a blow to owners. No obvious greed here, we believe, but it may contribute to a sense of falling fortunes among Millennials, and their sense of unfairness.

THE ELDERLY

Another generational victim of greed is the elderly. There is a whole ecosystem oriented to taking money from them. Again, some of this greed is quite hidden although, for instance, inflation acts like a tax and falls most heavily on the elder population. As money devalues,

---

[19]C. Cilliza "A Very Revealing Donald Trump Quote about Why He Ran for President," CNNPolitics, September 26, 2020.
[20]C. Lewis, "Right on the Money: The George W. Bush Profile," The Center for Public Integrity, July 8, 2003.
[21]"The Boomer Bust," *Wall Street Journal*, October 12, 2018, p. M8 K. Dore, "How soaring inflation may deliver a higher tax bill – especially for retirees," CNBC Personal Taxes, July 18, 2022.

those who must rely on savings suffer the most, while those who live primarily from earned income will see wages increase roughly in line with inflation.[22]

Other, quite pernicious, disadvantages for retirees lie in securities regulations. Many institutions, for example, Citibank, do not allow money in retirement accounts to be invested in inverse exchange traded funds (ETFs).[23] This rule prevents retirees from protecting their savings in the case of a stock market downturn. The rationale for this rule is apparently that some consider this class of ETFs more hazardous than simple equities. Really? The NASDAQ fell by a third over 2022, the Dow Jones Average almost 9%. So is an inverse ETF more dangerous than an actual loss??

Finally, there are many financial advisors who take advantage of the reduced litigiousness of seniors and tailor their services to take advantage of them. For instance, when there were trans-action fees for stock trades, some brokers "churned" accounts, trading stocks more frequently than optimal. As mentioned earlier, another means for taking advantage of seniors is por-traying some financial instruments as very safe, but then changing their strategies.[24] A great example is Charles Schwab Corporation's "Redi-Funds," which the firm positioned as a very safe short-term instrument, but then switched to real-estate investments which crashed. Largely, the seniors are the ones who suffer from this hidden greed.

While Millennials may have a cause to complain about the Boomers, all generations have less to complain about than the elderly. So, instead of being exploitive, they should follow three ethical principles which will benefit elders – and themselves – in the long run. The ethical principles include:[25]

---

[22]J. Hilsenrath and R. Wolfe "Inflation takes the Biggest Bite from the Middle," December 29, 2022, p. A1.

[23]An ETF is an "exchange traded fund" and usually includes a basket of stocks within it, so it behaves much like a stock. An "inverse" ETF will move in the opposite direction of a set of stocks. For instance, an inverse ETF will go up 10% when, for example, the S&P 500 goes down 10%.

[24]Y. Hayashi. "More Seniors Victimized by Financial Scams," *The Wall Street Journal*, January 25, 2019, p. A3.

[25]More, Ibid, Chapter VII, Section I.

- Respecting what others know

- Gratitude

- Looking forward

These principles serve us all well. In particular, "gratitude," which counters emotional disturbances such as anger. Anger is an increasingly common emotion, particularly toward elected officials.[26]

Not many generations have delivered desirable situations to their successor generations. Even the "Greatest Generation" (born in 1920s) were the architects of a war in Vietnam supporting the wrong side, at least as viewed from a democratic standpoint.[27] However, this generation served in the Second World War and correctly defended South Korea from invasion by an insane regime in North Korea. They also delivered a fairly robust economy.

So, on balance, generations are not created equally, nor is any generation perfect. This suggests all generations should exhibit some mercy toward other generations.[28]

The next chapter asks the question "what is greed?" and discusses it in greater depth. It provides a more detailed definition and explanation, and shows that greed's victims fall into a few recognizable categories – some undoubtedly including readers of this book.

[26]S. Lai, L. Broadwater and C. Huke "Surging Threats Put Lawmakers in Fearful Place," *New York Times*, October 2, 2022, p. 1.
[27]L. Logevall, *The Embers of War*, Random House, 2012, p. 194.
[28]Noema XII.

9

WHAT IS GREED HAVING FOR LUNCH?

Question: Where does greed come from?
How does knowing that help us?

> Some might ask whether the path is before us or within
> us. The answer is: Yes. We are both driven from within
> by our resident spirit and something outside calls forth
> the genius within us.
>
> Michael Meade (The Genius Myth)

In what situations do people feel an inclination to be greedy?
This chapter describes a few situations and why greed thrives in
those places. In a nutshell, it is because greed is a function of power.
Greed is usually reinforced by the social circle in which the greedy
individuals operate, and it makes them feel more powerful.

Before looking at concentrations of greed, consider the definition
and variations of greed. We have previously described the strategies
of greed, but have not looked closely at a definition or the threshold
that separates greed from ordinary ambition. The classical Greeks
considered greed at length and concluded it existed whenever
people attempted to exceed a number of modest standards. These
standards are:

- The transactional standard that a price must be at cost, but no more.[1]

- Wanting more than what is necessary for a household to survive.[2]

- Seeking an amount which shows a lack of restraint.[3]

- Improper acquisitions.[4]

- By references to history, and previous wealth.[5]

- Taking more than one's share.[6]

- Wanting so much that the rest of the polis (state) suffers.[7]

- Obtaining wealth from injustice or tyranny.[8]

- Obtaining wealth as a marker of social rank or an indication of power and relationship to broader society.[9]

Most of these standards set a modest threshold for greed. They reflect an agricultural society with (initially) not a lot of social layers. If we were to apply these standards to modern society, we might judge many people as being greedy. For instance, today most people seek "more than necessary for a household to survive." Of course, that does not render the old standards wrong, neither does it necessarily render more current standards exaggerated. It does suggest that greed is a function of the societal context.

---

[1]R. Balot, *Greed and Injustice in Classical Athens*, Princeton University Press, 2001, pp. 30 and 162.
[2]Ibid, p. 34.
[3]Ibid, p. 103. We interpret this standard means that one can infer the inner state from the behavior, and that rapaciousness shows lack of self-control.
[4]Ibid, pp. 244 and 85.
[5]Ibid, p. 57.
[6]Ibid, p. 27.
[7]Ibid, p. 39.
[8]Ibid, p. 23.
[9]Ibid, p. 12.

CAUSES OF GREED

More fundamentally, the Roman historian Livy said greed was an outcome, or product, of wealth, rather than an independent driver.[10] This makes sense, as most price judgments and determinations of what people want is contextual.[11] Further, wealth emboldens people. Not until one knows the comparison point or context is it clear whether a thing will be viewed as satisfying by a potential owner. If greed is excess wanting, then we need to know *what* is excessive. It must be based upon a standard such as existing wealth. This relationship is further supported by the other definitions above. If circumstances are modest, as they were before Athens expanded its empire, then the baseline is survival of one's family. As the society developed beyond subsistence farming, then more abstract bases for greed became relevant.

The scope of greed is broad. Aristotle says it includes money, honor, or safety. He also notes that greed's pleasures come not just from wealth, but from the competition for money, the pleasure of gain, and from getting more than one deserves.[12]

So where do these behaviors come from? The answer in many cases is that it comes from *within* the greedy themselves, and in other cases, it stems from social context. Today, we suspect, a lot of the influence comes from society, which, through the proliferation of electronic forms of media (social and otherwise), is much more aware of what is going on around it. In place of a strong classical teaching that one should want only what one needs, the majority of people in countries belonging to the Organization for Economic Cooperation and Development (OECD) believe that more is better. Most people judge their material success compared to their peer group. Greed emerges when they feel they are falling short. There are still some people – a minority – which are in the "content with enough" category. Religious communities, such as monasteries and convents, communes, and other enclaves of those who eschew amassing material goods, still exist.

---

[10]Ibid, p. 15. This means people ask "Is this more or less than I had before? Than others had?"
[11]R. Docters, *Contextual Pricing*, McGraw-Hill, 2011, pp. 33–45.
[12]Aristotle, Ibid.

Although these institutions may not have the influence of times past, they still demonstrate that a less materialistic view is still viable.

DARK SHADOWS OF GREED

Today, greed thrives in a number of situations, typically where the powerful and the weak coexist. For instance, drug cartels have begun to kill children as a means for intimidating authorities and the public.[13]

A 2015 news report on human trafficking in Mexico said that there was no resistance to the kidnapping of young women and girls in the town of Tenancingo because a majority of residents derived benefits from the trafficking ring.[14] Apparently, in this town, money papered over morality and ethics.

Human trafficking is clearly an example of unethical behavior. The victims are not accorded the freedom, respect, and rights they deserve. They are clearly regarded as objects, which violates Kant's principles. Perhaps more interesting is the ethical stance of the townsfolk who stand by and let the trafficking go on. According to both Professor More's and Kant's precepts, the uninvolved observers probably have no general obligations to the victims if they don't know them or don't have a relationship with them. But the observers may owe something to themselves. How can seeing underage women kidnapped and sent to life of sexual slavery be anything but wrong? Professor More writes: "Wherefore all pravity is repugnant to human Nature."[15,16] This behavior violates ethical rules.

When Bayer Pharmaceuticals was considering its pricing scale for health-care networks ("networks"), the company increased prices every year. Its popular contraceptives such as Yaz, Yasmin, Mirena, and others were required to make the network's offerings complete. It was also the case that the cost of any one group of drugs would not render the health network unviable. Therefore,

---

[13]L. Diaz, "Mexican Gunmen Target Children in Gruesome Drug War," Reuters, January 17, 2008.
[14]G. Seith, "Sex Trafficking: A Dark Side To the New World Order" Wall Street Journal, p. 1, May 17, 2000.
[15]"Captivity" is condemned by More in Chapter II, Section X.
[16]More, Ibid, Chapter II, Section V.

Bayer increased its prices every year, not sure of how high they could go.

The Bayer situation is far more subtle than human trafficking. The contraceptive pharmaceutical purchase agreements were made with knowledgeable companies and people. Ultimately, there was some economic damage to the health-care clients, as their annual fees must have gone up. The immediate transactions between Bayer and health plan providers were probably ethical for Bayer, but were they for health-care networks? Probably not. The health plan providers may not have fought hard enough for its client base. That is unethical. They may have said that they were negotiating strongly, but was it strongly enough? Did they use the full suite of negotiation tactics, such as understanding the other side, and sequencing demands so that they could do better? Mediocre negotiating tactics, may be unethical when the slacking party is negotiating for someone else's benefit, i.e., the health-care network is negotiating on behalf of its subscribers.[17] Typical shortfalls include failure to prepare fully for negotiations, e.g., most negoti-ators do not know precisely the structure of their opponent's compensation plans. Usually, the compensation structure for negotiators, somewhat removed from the results, is not draconian, and they are not punished for not performing strongly on any given negotiation.[18] It also provides guidance on what to be firm about, and what not. When a strong negotiation team is inserted into "business as usual" negotiations, the results can be dramatic.[19] So, lackadaisical negotiators are failing in their duties.

---

[17]There are many levels of negotiations. A good example of the strongest negotiation comes from the entertainment industry. In 2006, The Food Network did the full-court press against the cable companies, in some cases raising their prices by five-fold. This was despite their share of programming being quite small compared to other networks. The difference was determination and smarts.

[18]More also condemns complacency, Chapter IX, Section II.

[19]For instance, when The Food Network brought in Lynn Costantini to run its licensing negotiations in 2009, she developed systematic strategies to raise Food Network pricing by 500% (!). That was ethical, while the weak responses from Cable Networks may not have been.

PUBLIC EXAMPLES

Other examples of unethical choices depict a pattern in which the strong hurt the weak, typically at the behest of a broader public. The broader public is particularly indifferent to ethical lapses when the actions happen out of sight, whether intentionally hidden or not. Examples below showcase instances which led to very high prices. In both instances, the products sought were not essential to life, but were highly desired by consumers. In each case, the consumer had multiple choices including humane ones, but ignored those options:

Lobsters. As noted earlier, boiling humans or lobsters to death is inhumane and unethical. As a reminder, research by Queen's University shows lobsters suffer immense pain when being boiled. Is this justified regarding a commodity which 30 years ago was not valued and called a "trash" fish? There is a simple solution: kill the lobster before placing in boiling water. This may actually be healthier for the diner, as no pain hormones are released into the lobster's bloodstream and communicated to the diner. In determining the greedy actor in this situation, the diner controls through demand. Without demand, the problem would not exist.

Eye Makeup.

For fear that users would apply eye makeup in ways not recommended by cosmetics companies, the companies for many years subjected millions of albino rabbits to the "Draize Test." This test was designed to assess the toxicity of chemicals and mixtures used in eye makeup and the potential to cause eye irritation or damage. The test caused painful irritation and, frequently, blindness. Rabbits scream during the test. The rabbits are killed within a few weeks after the tests.[20] No government regulation requires this test. Most US cosmetics companies (Avon, Revlon, L'Oréal) say they have stopped using this test. However, Chinese manufacturers, which sell products in the United States, still use the test.

---

[20] "Do Companies Still Test on Live Animals?" *Scientific American*, August 6, 2008.

Pork and Veal.

Only slightly less horrific is the treatment of pigs and calves. It happens out of the sight and control of diners. Both animals are subjected to close confinement and pain. Pigs used for breeding spend almost their entire adult life confined to gestation crates about the size of their bodies. They cannot turn around or lie down comfortably. These sows are impregnated repeatedly until they are considered "spent," and then sent to slaughter.[21] This treatment, like that of the cosmetic industry's rabbits, is legal. As it occurs out of sight and pigs are not as cuddly as rabbits, stopping the practice will require more effort. While the pork industry is clearly engaging in the unethical, it's less clear that diners bear the same level of responsibility, but clearly some responsibility.

The illustrations below marked in dark tones display the most influential part of the chain in these two examples (Fig. 9.1):

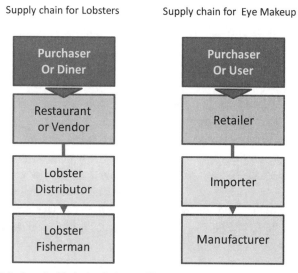

Fig. 9.1. Supply Chain for Lobsters/Eye Makeup.

---

[21]Pigs, The Humane League, 2022. They note that pigs are smarter than dogs and can play simple video games, so that this cannot be distinguished based on intelligence of the victim.

The key questions are:

- What are the ethical obligations of diners consuming lobsters which will die a horrible death as a result of their demand?

- What are the obligations of women buying cosmetics from companies which continue to torture rabbits?

Clearly, most people have concluded – if they have thought about it at all – that they bear no responsibility. They have become habituated.[22]

Habituation is not typically an ethical excuse. Psychiatrists have found that psychopaths feel no guilt about their actions. Similarly, the repetition of the act probably makes it easier for consumers to brush aside ethical considerations. But consumers have low-effort options, such as demanding that lobsters be killed before boiling. Consumers can choose an eye makeup manufactured without inhumane testing. (Men can ask questions of women about their makeup, also.)

So, the answer to "What is greed having for lunch?" is: The Weak. This is particularly true where the bad act is repeated and people become habituated.

Where does one find greed and unethical acts? Usually, you find it at the junction of power and some desirable asset like money or beauty. The trail gets hotter when there is previous evidence of bad acts by "the usual suspects."[23]

Of course, as we saw in Chapter 1 of this book, it is not always easy to identify the unethical and cruel. To do so, it is helpful to look inside oneself. Kate Pierson, songwriter and lead singer of the rock group the B-52s, said in an interview "We write songs which come from the truth. Listening to the radio does not give you that." She gets her inspiration from the "truth."[24] Professor More and Kant suggest much the same. Ethics in many cases stems from internal observance.[25]

---

[22]A. Goldfarb, "Why Re-watching Your Favorite TV Show Is Good for You," *Time*, May 17, 2022.
[23]Captain Renault giving orders toward the end of the movie *Casablanca*.
[24]Interview with K. Pierson, "Remembering The B-52's Sound with Kate Pierson and Wife Monica Coleman," Studio 10, April 20, 2020.
[25]R. Scruton, *Kant: A Very Short Introduction*, Oxford University Press, p. 34.

SECTION V

ETHICAL STRATEGY

10

GREED FIGHTS BACK!

Question: Is greedy behavior overcome by shunning greed?

> The most common way people give up their power is by thinking they don't have any.
>
> Alice Walker

Sadly, greed does not always retreat when confronted, and it can be complex. For instance, when hackers invaded the US White House computer system in 2016, instead of disappearing when exposed, they fought back, installing new malware as soon as their older implants were neutralized.

"It was basically hand to hand combat," said Richard Ledgett, the deputy director of the National Security Agency. "The hackers (likely Russian) wanted to prove they could go, and stay, anywhere in the American government network."[1]

Greed will fight back if it has the power and believes it can evade retribution. This is logical: self-interest by the greedy is common. And when greedy behavior is successful, there is no impetus to change strategy. Often greed creates a network which makes retribution and eradication difficult.

---

[1] D. Sanger, "We Can't Stop the Hackers," *The New York Times*, June 17, 2018, p. 14.

NETWORKS

The nature of greed networks is diverse. Some examples, which may qualify as evil in addition to greedy, include: a famous example of a protective network that gave Jeffrey Epstein confidence that his predatory behavior toward young women would avoid punishment. Epstein sought to have himself photographed with Bill Clinton, Donald Trump, and other public figures. He claimed he advised Elon Musk on Tesla strategy. He escaped prosecution in Florida and claims elsewhere were downplayed. It appeared that Epstein had the benefit of friends who did not want their own behavior exposed, so they intervened on his behalf.[2] In effect, Epstein created a useful network of *quid pro quo*, augmented by wiring some $350,000 to potential witnesses.[3]

A prosaic example, lacking celebrities, of greed is human trafficking. These networks are extensive and dangerous. One example, already mentioned, is the prostitution pipeline from Tenancingo, Mexico, to the United States. The network is remarkably broad, involving many wrongdoer participants. There, young women are kidnapped and trafficked. There is no broad resistance to this because "... young boys are taught that [the sex trade] is not only okay, but this is how you make money. This is your path in life." Once the women are in the US trafficking ring members hand out cards with a cell phone number. Customers can call and have a girl delivered. Investigators say the young women are transported around the country by a broad network of drivers acting as guards.[4]

Some networks of greed are even more broad-based. For instance, many Americans hold a negative view of the stock market – with good cause. Observers say that inside trading is pervasive and that regulators and the Department of Justice ignores it. "The... amount of opportunistic abuse that exists under the current

---

[2]J. Stewart, "Epstein Boasted of Dirt on the Rich and Powerful," *The New York Times*, August 13, 2019, p. B1.
[3]B. Weiser, "Tale of Bribery in Call to Deny Bail for Epstein," *The New York Times*, July 13, 2019, p. A1.
[4]A. Brennan, "Prostitution Pipeline to the US Begins in Tenancingo, Mexico," Wbur.org, June 30, 2014.

system [is] egregious," said Professor Daniel Taylor, head of the Wharton Forensic Analytics Lab at the University of Pennsylvania.[5]

Not unexpectedly, there are myriad abuses. The regulations are set up to disadvantage smaller traders. While routine trades are carefully monitored, trades outside the markets are not. Is this fair?

Stock market manipulation is not just unfair but also unethical (and often illegal). It violates Noema XIV which says that actions (like trading) are not ethical when they prejudice a third party. This makes sense, but is sharply at odds with the ethics of Wall Street.

GREED FIGHTS BACK

What to do about this? You must first understand that taking action will be difficult and there may be reprisals. As mentioned, greed often fights back. Some examples are as follows:

- The US embarked on a massive monitoring of citizen communications in 2010. Julian Assange, an Australian editor and founder of WikiLeaks, aided by various National Security Agency staff, revealed the monitoring which was later ruled illegal by Federal Courts. Although many considered Assange's action a positive act, the US government declared him a threat to national security and accused him of violating the US Espionage Act. In 2022, Assange was imprisoned in the United Kingdom pending a legal battle over extradition to the United States. He enjoys international support from various newspapers, the ACLU, and an Australian parliamentary group.[6]

- A report in Linkedin.com/pulse described how a supervisor rated one employee highly because he was highly productive. Other supervisors criticized the supervisor, who, because of his forceful advocacy, was fired.[7]

---

[5]L. Vaughan, "Most Americans Today Believe the Stock Market is Rigged, and they're Right," Bloomberg.com, September 29, 2021, p. 5.
[6]E. Wasserman, "Julian Assange and the War on Whistle-Blowers," *The New York Times*, April 27, 2019, p. A23.
[7]J. Haden, "I Did the Right Thing and Still Got Fired: My Cautionary Tale," Linkedin.com/pulse, October 24, 2014.

- The CEO of Volkswagen moved the company from air-cooled engines and the number six market position in Europe to modern water-cooled engines and the number one position in the market. Despite having saved the company, the chairman was fired shortly after this accomplishment.[8] His aggressive management had alienated the unions and board members caved into the union demands. A similar fate befell Lee Iacocca at Ford after he boosted sales with new models, but in the process alienated the Chair Henry Ford II.[9]

Perhaps the essential difference between managers who run afoul of their peers or supervisors is that some managers are focused on progress and improvement while other managers are focused on convenience, promotions, and avoiding strife. This can take place at any level in the organization. Self-serving managers who reach the top ranks often are so self-assured that they believe their approach to management is best and they have the power to insulate themselves from criticism as discussed in the previous chapter.[10] A smug greed.

How to defend against this kind of greed? To begin with, don't rely on broad institutional goals as these goals are secondary to many people. In 2018, New Jersey Family Court Judge James Troiano rejected prosecutors who sought to charge a 16-year-old youth in adult court. The youth was accused of raping a 16-year-old intoxicated girl at a pajama party and recording it on his cell phone. Judge Troiano said the youth came from a good family and had good test scores. The judge said prosecutors should have told the girl and her family that bringing charges would wreck the boy's life.

A year later, the judge's ruling was overturned by an appellate court which excoriated Troiano for not applying the law and for

---

[8]S. Guyon, "Getting The Bugs Out At VW In six years, Ferdinand Piech has turned VW into one of the world's strongest car companies. Can he sustain it?" *Fortune*, March 29, 1999. Piech was fired in 2015. Note that we are not saying Dr Piech was nice or overall ethical, merely that he saved the company and Noema XV say this was ethical.

[9]"The Day in History, Henry Ford II Fires Lee Iacocca," www.History.com, January 27, 2020.

[10]Time article on psychosis.

giving preferential treatment to the youth.[11] Clearly the judge had a greater sense of alliance with the defendant, than the law, and especially not the victim. The case was an example of a member of a certain social class defending another member of a similar "good" social class. Such an affinity is powerful and represents a sort of group greed at the expense of others. This might also apply to any number of other groups who rally to defend each other.[12]

DEFENSE STRATEGY

So, what should be your strategy if you are on the other side of such a divide? We have addressed tactics earlier in the book, but tactics are not the same as a strategy. The first, and perhaps greatest, commentator on (military) strategy, Prussian General Carl von Clausewitz, declared:

War does not consist of a single instantaneous blow.[13]

Defense, including defense against greed, is an art. In the military, some generals have been known as defensive experts who were able to hold off superior forces well beyond what could have been expected. These experts employed an arsenal of tactics along with judicious timing and nuanced maneuvers.[14]

So, what strategies can be used to thwart greedy initiatives? We have already described defensive tactics which start with an ethical

---

[11]L. Ferre-Sadurni, "He is Accused of Rape, But Has a 'Good Family'," *The New York Times*, July 3, 2019, p. A1.

[12]S. Suranovic, "Distinguishing Self-Interest from Greed: Ethical Constraints and Economic Efficiency," George Washington University, October, 2019.

[13]C. von Clausewitz, *On War*, BN Publishing, 2007, p. 14. President/General Eisenhower recommended the same thing in his final State of the Union address in 1961.

[14]One famous example of a defensive genius was German General Gotthard Heinrici. Gen. Heinrici was able to win a number of defensive battles, including the Battle of Seelow Heights where he held off 40 Russian divisions numbering about 1–1.5 million soldiers, with his two divisions numbering less than 110,000. After the war he was given an assignment in the US Army. Another great defensive general was French General Jean de Lattre de Tassigny, who was Commander of French forces in Vietnam and succeeded in repulsing North Vietnamese forces. Only after he succumbed to cancer did the tide turn against France. See F. Longevall, *Embers of War*, Random House, 2012, pp. 255–287.

principle. But there are others. A powerful alternative is *multiple reinforcing* strategies. What does that mean?

An example can be drawn from the leading South African company which leases aerial lift and construction equipment to open pit mineral excavations: The industry is very cost-conscious, so knowing specific site costs is the key to winning business. An incumbent equipment lessor will know what the costs are to service a specific site – the nature of the soil and rock faces, what that means for building scaffolding and moving equipment, and site maintenance. A potential new aerial lift lessor will not know this key information.

Thus, a defensive strategy by the incumbent is (1) to divide the business into two halves: short term rentals, which address the fluctuation of demand over time. (2) Longer term rentals which address the base-load needs.

When there are short-term upticks, then the equipment are contracted by short-term leases. From a cost point of view, one might expect the short-term lease to be more expensive, e.g., from bringing in and setting up equipment. However, the lessor strategically charges less on short-term rentals. This means that any challenger cannot learn the costs of the site, and cannot underbid the incumbent on the short-term rentals because the incumbent has already priced these too low to challenge.

Blocking challengers from any short-term leases helps shield critical information about the costs of long-term leases. The strategy works very well and keeps profits high.[15] Thus, a multilevel strategy works to defend leasing business better than any single part strategy.

Drawing from this commercial example, we believe that the best ethical strategies rely on a number of elements or tools to avoid harm from *unethical initiatives*. These tools build upon each other

---

[15]This strategy by the lessor does not violate any of the Noema, with the possible exception of Noema 12 which highlights the need for sincerity and clarity. This could mean that candor is required to partners. However, competitors are not partners, and the Noema make clear by its absence that there is no general obligation. In fact, Noema I could be read as a charter to compete (albeit ethically).

to thwart greed. A few examples illustrate the options, each characterized by a core thought:

1. Vigilance.

   To combat the unethical, you must be aware of prospective unethical initiatives – and take action as needed:

   • Increasing violence in US schools has led some teachers to arm themselves. In Florida, 45 out of 74 school districts employ school staff who essentially are armed guardians.[16] This was driven by events, rather than a desire by teachers. This also was fueled by the neglect and indifference of school administrations which had failed to install doors which locked automatically upon closing or to hire police to be on campus.

   • In 2018, Niek Hoogervorst, an assistant professor at Rotterdam School of Management reported that a study of managers revealed that most managers were oblivious to the unethical.[17] Because most people take their ethical cues from context, they are particularly susceptible to networks of greed or neglect. A network of greed may include a wealthy or an aggressive organization.

     The counter to a network of greed is to be smarter. For instance, a significant portion of identity theft comes in the form of what appears to be a legitimate email or a legitimate website. However, if you learn to spot the subtle signs of fraud – odd sender addresses – or use available resources to verify the other party, you can prevent being victimized.[18]

2. Do not accept an unfair situation.

   The Noemata suggest we owe ourselves justice and should pursue the greatest good with the greatest zeal.[19] And "that to

---

[16]S. Merevos, "Armed. And Ready to Teach Kindergarten," *The New York Times*, Sunday, July 31, 2022, p. A1.

[17]N. Hoogevorst, Why do unethical practices go unpunished in business? HRZone, October 11, 2008.

[18]"Security: Staying Safe from Identify Theft," *The Week*, August 30, 2019, p. 33.

[19]Noemata XXII and XXIII.

bear ignominy… was a commission to do evil."[20] We live in a world full of greed and evil. Here are two examples of this and two different reactions:

- Cheerleaders for the Washington Redskins professional football team were flown to Costa Rica for a photo shoot. Upon arrival, Redskin officials collected their passports. Some of the cheerleaders were asked to go topless and some were told to entertain some of the male club sponsors. They were told this was "mandatory." Several of the cheerleaders wept. None flatly refused. None of the cheerleaders, who were underpaid and had little job security, later filed suit for a hostile work environment, apparently because they feared they would be fired.[21] Clearly, the ethical mandate was to be firm and seek justice.[22]

- In contrast, parents of children murdered and wounded at the Sandy Hook Elementary School in Connecticut, filed suit against *Infowars* website leader Alex Jones. Jones claimed the reports of the shooting were a hoax, and the event was staged by the parent and the government.[23] In 2022, after years of harassment by Jones supporters, the parents were awarded $965 million in actual damages and $45.2 million in punitive damages.[24] This was a positive outcome for fighting the falsehoods.

3. To be an effective communicator.

   - Often, the very act which is unethical is not revealed by those who are aware of it because they feel it would be unethical to provide the details. This is wrong. While there would be issues with exploiting photographs for commercial purposes, there are none in using them to prevent future wrongful acts.

---

[20]More, *supra*, Chapter XI, Section X.
[21]J. Macur, "For Cheerleaders, a Trip Had Unwelcome Guests," *The New York Times*, May 3, 2018, p. A1.
[22]Several other football teams were sued for similar issues by their cheerleaders.
[23]E. Williamson, "Fabulist Will Face Testimony from Sandy Hook Parents," *The New York Times*, July 26, 2022, p. A18.
[24]A. Nguyn, "Alex Jones Files for Bankrupcy after Juries Award Sandy Hook Parents Almost $1.5B," The Texas Tribune, December 2, 2022.

Thus the photos of children killed during school shootings have been effective in campaigns to support antigun legislation, and pictures of slaves disfigured by their owners helped spark abolitionist movements.[25]

- Humor is rarely used. Prof. More endorses humor as a sign of good ethics.[26] "The Colbert Report" was effective at exposing and underscoring negative actions by President Bush and other leaders. However, there were few specific action proposals in the show. Another example of humor was the "Birds Aren't Real" movement among twenty-somethings. This was a parody of older peoples' claims that various problems such as environmental deterioration are not real. The founder of the movement describes it as "fighting lunacy with lunacy."[27]

- Conventional channels for communication often do not work to promote change. This is, in part, because the forces of stasis know to expect these messages and are familiar with the strategies of countering the messages. For instance, employers expect to face whistleblowers, and have the best responses prepared.

4. Be sincere.
- While Facebook has spent billions of dollars to try to win back trust, to little avail, Starbucks was instantly applauded when it offered to pay the costs of transport for employees in antiabortion states seeking abortions out of state.[28] Apparently, people can sense sincerity and benevolence.

Interventions need to be strategic and smart. Dumb does not do well against greed, especially groups of greedy people. Also, interventions should not be inhibited by rules designed to help the greedy. For instance, victims of crimes often fail to contact the

---

[25]E. Williamson, "Would Photographs of the Bodies Change Views?" *The New York Times*, May 30, 2022, p. A1.
[26]Chapter VI, Sections II and IV.
[27]T. Lorenz, "A Gen Z-led 'Conspiracy' with Wings, and a Wink, Takes on Misinformation," *The New York Times*, December 10, 2021, p. A1.
[28]L. Foreman, Facebook, *The Wall Street Journal*.

police, or give all the facts, for fear being victimized again by the perpetrators. Newspapers can shape the news erroneously, even in unintended ways.[29] For instance, after the Sandy Hook mass murder of school children, one family had an open-coffin viewing. They believed the impact would propel other parents to become more active in preventing similar tragedies.[30] However, the impact was minimized because the media did not show the coffin, likely because the press in the US has long self-censored to avoid accusations of sensationalism. There also is a concern that showing such photographs or videos resulted in fewer readers/viewers, and less advertising revenue. The smashed desks and windows inside the school were not shown because the journalists were denied access. Again: why?

Communication of the unpleasant has proven to drive public opinion. There are many examples – battlefield scenes of the Vietnam War, abuse and murder of minorities, and the killing of George Floyd to name just a few. Of course, there are many not involved in events who do not want to see such images, and they have support from various people (in public office, or running relief organizations, or others) to prevent the media from obtaining those images.[31] Some suggest a simple solution for the oversensitive: turn the page/channel. That priority is consistent with Noema XIX which says it is "better that one person lives less delicately if it helps those living a calamitous life."[32]

Any intervention must be strategic and well considered. The account of a manager who was fired after supporting one employee *supra* represents poor strategy. He did not pick and cultivate his allies, he cut no deals, and he failed to engage his boss. That is not recommended.

No matter how righteous a cause, stupidity is usually fatal to success unless the goal is very modest. An amusing military analogy comes from the British Royal Navy. During World War I, an

---

[29]For instance, the *New Haven Register* converted one reporter's account of a robbery from "a tall black man" to "a man." Not helpful.
[30]"Would Photographs of the Bodies Change Views," *The New York Times*, May 30, 2022 p. A1.
[31]A. Roche, "*A Proposal to Curb Access to Photos of Murder Victims* [Senate Bill 1512]," The Texas Tribune, May 9, 2013.
[32]More, Ibid.

Admiral decided to defend his port against U-Boats by equipping a number of motor launches with gunny sacks and hammers. The plan was that sailors, upon spotting periscopes, would rush out to U-Boats, place a gunny sack over the periscope, and then hammer it into submission. This did not work.[33]

Stupidity is generally a good way to provoke undesirable behavior, to the point where it is difficult to assign blame. For instance, a leading IT implementation firm recently bid for a project with a top-4 New York bank. They estimated that the project should cost $6 million, but the bank refused to award more than $3 million. When the project was not complete for $3 million, the bank found that it needed to further fund the project. The delays in this process increased the total cost to the bank to $8 million.[34] In this case, the greed of wanting a $6 million dollar project done for $3 million cost the bank $2 million.

CHANGE MANAGEMENT

As noted previously, to address greed, one must recognize it. And not everyone does. As a recent organizational behavior article noted: "managers don't recognize greed when it happens."[35]

This means vigilance is paramount. At the outset, managers must know what they are looking for. This requires training of two sorts: (1) General training concerning ethical principles and (2) Familiarity with the likely forms of greed.[36] This training is not easy.

Some managers will see this sort of training as trivial and a waste of time. Even more concerning, some managers will see this as a potential obstacle to their preferred mode of interactions with workers and customers. In both cases, they will fail to recognize and act upon instances of greed.

To make the training effective, it must be seen as authoritative, legitimate, and consequential. The first of these descriptors is

---

[33]G. Regan, *Naval Blunders*, Guinness Publishing, 1993.
[34]Confidential company records for 2020.
[35]"Greed Reflects a Failure of Leadership," Knowledge at Wharton, June 20, 2008.
[36]M. Dde BVries, "Seven Signs of the Greed Syndrome," INSEAD Knowledge, August 17, 2021.

perhaps the easiest. We have found that the age and specificity of Professor More's ethical summary commands respect. Some will ask if it is still relevant, but that can be addressed through a sample of modern utilitarianism citations.

It must be perceived as legitimate. Usually, the most ethically challenged employees will contest new standards. This makes sense, as often they are experienced in flaunting existing rules. They also may know of senior managers' past ethical lapses and transgressions and ask why they should act differently.

This requires some of the standard cornerstones of change management:

- A declaration that change has really come. This typically means a declaration from the company president or CEO.

- A symbol of change. This can be painful. A good example can be drawn from the experience of AT&T Canada. During the 1990s, the company was losing money. At the same time, some of their clients were harassing female AT&T salespeople. The CEO, William Catucci, warned the clients to stop and, when they did not, he cut off the accounts. This was painful, but it sent a strong message.

- Incentives are important. These should be both sanctions and positive incentives. One leading media firm provided incentives by offering extra executive support, and other impactful benefits such as greater discounting authority to sales reps who might otherwise be tempted to cut corners. Management was sufficiently in touch with the situation in the field that reps who cut corners could be identified. Of course, some reps preferred to continue with the unethical practices despite signs of change. For those individuals, management audited sales reports. All were warned they had violated conditions of employment, and a second offense would result in being fired. Some were, not long afterward.

Before change can begin, there is a more basic question: does the top management, or the point person, believe that ethical behavior is a good strategy? This is critical because an insincere presenter will be sniffed out immediately. For instance, missing meetings and failing to make affirmative comments can be telling.[37] Hence the admonition from Aristotle that "Learners must believe."[38]

Peeling the onion back one more layer, you may have to convince a top manager of the efficacy of change. That may not be easy, although resistance (even if masked) is a telltale sign that future action will be required. How to convince?

1. Senior management is no different than rank and file in that they are open to incentives to change.[39] The incentives need to be well tailored, have a difference and not be insulting. In 1994, the CEO of BellSouth repeatedly engineered major shifts in the wireline and wireless strategies by offering strong incentives to each divisional president.

2. Proof of concept by trial is a good tool, although not as effective to overcome long-standing practices. There have been numerous comparison trials in which different practices are run side by side. When the comparisons are exact, and there is an incentive for improvement, they can work. Comparing geographic territories has worked well for assessing salesforce initiatives. These must be fueled by an incentive, such as cash awards or other substantial benefits, or the different outcomes will be ignored. For instance, at one software company the outcomes were ignored because the managers who refused to employ the practices were successful anyway, if not as much.

3. Note that a trial is appropriate for testing the details of the practice, not for broader ethical frameworks. For instance, if an ethics audit turns up two ethical problems, it may be that they are very different in severity. Two examples:
   • An outside plant crew assigned to dig a trench between two sections of a plant digs energetically on Friday and then returns on Monday to discover that rains have collapsed the

---

[37]R. McMillan, "Twitter Whistleblower Is Famed Ex-Hacker, System Security Sleuth," *Wall Street Journal*, August 25, 2033, p. B2.
[38]More, ibid, Chapter II, Section IX.
[39]M. Palmquist, "Want More Ethical Employees? Give 'Em a Nudge" *Stategy & Business*, issue 89, Winter 2017, p. 100.

trench. A manager who was experienced in working in rainy climate had suggested not to dig before a two-day gap because the trench was not shored up. This advice was ignored. Apparently "Not Invented Here" (NIH) was in operation.

This squarely violated Noema VI, which says that one should accept suggestions from people more knowledgeable, but there was relatively little harm done.

- AOL once made it very difficult for subscribers to cancel. As a result, many customers spent hours in the process of canceling, and often calls were dropped before cancellation was completed. This violated Noemata I ("grateful [and] pleasant" is good), and XXIII ("... a man may so behave himself, as that was own by acquisition or donation, may of right cease to be his own."). This violation was more fundamental and broader in scope. There should be no field trial (even if one were possible) because senior management needs to correct it.

COUNTERING THE UNETHICAL

Countering an unethical initiative is often more than just employing a single Noema. The core of resisting the unethical is to be strategic and to be ethical. As Professor More noted, it is fitting to call "virtue rather a power than a habit."[40]

This is necessary because the unethical have become skilled at executing their strategies. Look no further than *Fox News* political commentator Tucker Carlson. Carlson is a talented television commentator who is known for baseless racism, denial that COVID-19 vaccines are effective, and the reasons for various shootings.[41] Carlson cannot be called ethical because he neglects

---

[40]More, Chapter III, Section I. Virtue is analogous to valor and good fortune in battle.

[41]N. Confessore, "What to Know about Tucker Carlson's Rise," *The New York Times*, April 30, 2022.

"the study and improvement… to all men." And does not display "a forcible restraint upon Lust and Anger."[42]

Some individuals use greed to achieve their goals. In October 2020, a white curator named Nancy Spencer was forced out of her job at The Guggenheim Museum in New York City. She was forced out following a bitter campaign launched by a Black activist named Chaédria LaBouvier, who said Spencer was racist. The furor centered on an exhibition of work by Black artist Jean-Michel Basquiat at the museum in which LaBouvier was curating as a guest curator.

An article in *The Atlantic* detailed a multilayered clash at the museum.[43] LaBouvier had worked to have the painting exhibited at the Williams College Museum of Art. After that she looked to move onto bigger and better things. She was invited by Spencer to curate a Basquiat exhibition at the Guggenheim. LaBouvier portrayed Spencer as seeking to "co-opt" credit for the painting's exhibition. LaBouvier skillfully worked social media and invoked the George Floyd killing to attack management at the Guggenheim, and apparently placed the Board of Directors under pressure for "failing" to fully pursue racial justice. The museum forced Spencer out to defuse LaBouvier's complaints. This rewarded LaBouvier's ambitious campaign which was based on false claims of racism.[44] Other institutions had faced complaints from LaBouvier, but had dismissed them. For example, the BBC dismissed LaBouvier's complaints about a documentary involving Basquiat.[45]

None of this is surprising. This is just another example of how greed is weaponized and the user then denies using it. These actions exemplify greed because they are extreme and involve the destructive use of labels to obtain advantage. LaBouvier seems to have prevailed because of the relative lack of interest in the facts by the Guggenheim management and their Board. We see this as an example of how evil succeeds when good men do nothing.[46]

---

[42]More, Chapter III, Section III.

[43]H. Lexis, "The Scapegoat," *The Atlantic*, November 22, 2022, p. 58.

[44]Ibid, p. 66, October 8, 2020. A report commissioned by the museum found no evidence of racism on the part of Nancy Spencer.

[45]Ibid, p. 64.

[46]A thought often attributed to Edmund Burke, but said to be misattributed. Nonetheless relevant.

In both cases, there was a breakdown of language. Tucker Carlson and Chaédria LaBouvier used words and labels for impact. People say things, some of it untrue, for different reasons. We know of an instance where a midlevel manager at a large telephone company was asked if he had started a particular project. He answered affirmatively and so senior management was satisfied. When asked later why he said yes, when he knew nothing had happened, the manager said: "Well, since it was impossible to have begun, I assumed the question reflected that, so I answered in the way it must have been asked."

There are two types of dialogs: those where words/labels float free of concrete meaning, and those where the connection to specific facts ensures meaningful words. See Fig. 10.1 below. It represents the two types of situations observed in different situations. In one, words and labels are meaningful. In the other, they mean little and simply echo back and forth not connected to real events.

Professor More was aware of the secondary and linguistic impacts of an evil deed. In Noema VI, he suggested we refrain from

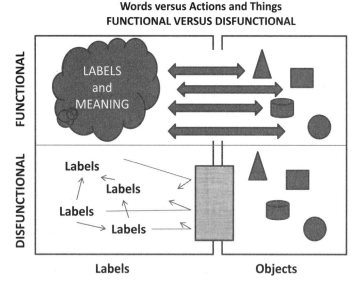

Fig. 10.1. Words Versus Actions and Things.

doing bad things if they prejudice a third party. In the case of the Guggenheim, the management destroyed the career of a senior curator. This is not an isolated incident. One CEO has said that he stopped offering suggestions or counseling to female employees because of fear of harassment charges. He said he opted for demanding more work, rather than smarter work.[47]

---

[47]CEO of a $500MM/yr. international services firm.

11

STUPIDITY, FAULT, AND ETHICS

Question: Does joining a mass movement soften ethical rules?

A lie doesn't become truth, wrong doesn't become right, and evil doesn't become good, just because it's accepted by a majority.

Booker T. Washington

Being part of a great movement is satisfying and comforting to the participants. In many endeavors of life, being part of a movement makes success more likely, and participants believe that there is someone who has done more thinking about it.[1] Indeed, group consensus is more likely to succeed than a stupid minority.[2]

But suppose you are not stupid? Is it wise to trust others with your ethical judgments? Especially over the long term? Crowd instincts tend to be more short-term and often unwise. Some examples of groupthink with ethical consequences include:

- Uneconomic ways to "save money." Surprisingly, many people are fixated on the price level, so they are fooled by a low price tag, although more expensive alternatives are of better quality or last longer, making the alternatives the right purchase choice.

[1] J. Surowiecki, *The Wisdom of Crowds*, Anchor 2005.
[2] D. Hamada, M. Nakayama and J. Saiki, Wisdom of crowds and collective decision-making in a survival situation with complex information integration, *Cognitive Research Journal*, 2020.

Examples include appliances whose purchase prices have been lowered, but have shorter working lifespans. This poses the question of whether it is ethical for sellers to use the tactic of low price tag with higher lifetime costs?

- Failure to use experts when that can save money. As an example, architect fees usually amount to 2% of a house's construction cost. This amounts to a fraction of the savings an architect can contribute to a project, such as an earlier completion date, the ability to identify a broader range of components for the lowest cost, and not inconsequentially, avoiding issues with municipal building and zoning departments. Should builders recommend the use of architects to save their clients' money? Yes. Noema VI would support the seeking of more experienced help.

  While this may seem an odd ethical mandate, promoted by the local trade union, it makes ethical sense. Reasons to refuse expert help are overwhelmingly negative. They might include exaggerated ego, refusing to acknowledge shortcomings. This is a good example of where ethics exists without overlapping with morals of law.

- Making choices based on the wrong criteria. For example, an eye surgeon has noted that some patients choose their hospital based on the length of the taxi ride, a weak criterion in light of the seriousness of surgery. How forcefully should a professional guide patients or clients away from bad choices?

- Making choices based upon news media sources quoting famous or wealthy people instead of seeking bona fide, but perhaps boring, expert opinion.[3] What is the obligation of the media?

- Relying upon a puzzling popular sentiment that "family-owned" farms must be more humane, and the products therefore must be healthier. While some family farms are likely more humane, some are not. Horizon Organic, the world's largest organic dairy brand, has dropped some family-owned farms because the

---

[3] A. Dao, "Money Talks," *The New Philosopher*, August–October 2018, p. 78. Gives example of tax suggestions by billionaires.

farms were not allowing cow's access to pastures and other amenities.[4] What duty and role do consumers have to counter stereotypes which may obscure inhumane conditions?

Perhaps surprisingly, a lot of stupid choices are unethical. The harm caused by poor choices affects others, and violates Noemata XIV and XV. Those who make poor choices ignore Professor More's guidance to listen to people who have greater familiarity with a problem,[5] such as *Consumer Reports* magazine, which publishes an array of recommendations ranging from cars to appliances and other home products.[6]

Do others have an obligation to help the stupid, and combat stupidity? There is no direct answer to that in *Enchiridion Ethicum*, but More does emphasize that "Fools" have a right to happiness and often being of "a moderate estate"[7] they can evade some of the ethical hazards of wealth.

Stupidity and unethical behavior is not confined to the marketplace. After the COVID-19 pandemic exploded in 2020, violence against Asian residents of US cities increased.[8] Blaming US Asians for the COVID-19 epidemic, which emerged from China, was a form of associative, but groundless, logic. Some of these protestors, ironically, refused to protect themselves by wearing masks or getting vaccinated. In addition to being illogical, this is unethical. Noema VI advises to avoid "speculative ignorance" and to engage in the "pursuit of truth."[9]

WHY?

Any assessment of those making stupid decisions begins with a question: Why? Why do they do this?

---

[4]Animal Welfare Institute, Winter 2021, vol. 70, Number 4, p. 22.
[5]Noema VI.
[6]Rarely is the CU recommendation the best seller.
[7]H. More, Enchiridion Ethicum, Chapter II, section XII.
[8]"Rising Against Asian Hate: One Day in March" premiered on Monday, October 17, 2022 at 9 p.m. on THIRTEEN, pbs.org/RisingAgainstAsianHate.
[9]More, Chapter V, Section VI.

In some cases, they genuinely may not be up to the task of thinking through decisions. However, in quite a few cases, egos are involved. Hubris clouds judgment. Some of these individuals may already believe that they are always right and so act to preserve this persona.[10]

Such a belief is a form of greed. This particularly applies to consumers.

Consumers happily dig into their food rationalizing the conditions for animals, which end up as their meals, whether it is fish farming, confinement of breeder pigs, or force feeding of ducks to produce foie gras.[11] Ignorance plays a role. Too few consumers of tuna know that the "Dolphin-Safe" seal comes in two versions. The colorful seal means what it always has meant – protection certified by National Oceanic and Atmospheric Administration's Seafood Inspection Program that care is taken not to catch and suffocate dolphins in the mile-long tuna nets. The black and white seal is less strict, and dolphins are killed. This is in accordance with legislation passed later. Consumers who do not look into these differences are being lazy and unethical.

Inside companies, greed takes various forms by managers who are essentially investing with the company's money. It can be a form of "put option." For example, if a senior manager assigns a more junior manager responsibility for a project and the project fails, then the senior manager can blame the junior manager and justify elimination of project staff. If the project succeeds, then the manager will claim some of the credit. Of course, in some companies, assigning blame or claiming credit may be difficult, but it happens frequently.

Of course, this won't work in a firm where key information, good and bad, gets reported up the line. While not good for shareholders, the "put option" approach is seen by some managers as a good career strategy.[12] Unless the project failure takes down the entire company, the managers can blame others for failures and claim credit for successes for themselves.

---

[10]M. Alvesson and A. Spicer, *The Stupidity Paradox*, Profile Books 2016, pp. 150–151.
[11]See "Seaspiracy", Netflix, 2021. Directed by Ali Tabrizi.
[12]Alvesson, Ibid.

All of this, of course, is bad management. If responsibilities and the risks of failure were clearly delineated, it would not be possible for anyone in the chain of command to shun responsibility. Similarly, if management had a solid reporting chain, and a rigorous incentive structure for success, individuals would be appropriately rewarded.[13]

The major cause of poor management and the misattribution of credit and blame occurs because of "delayering." The idea is to save money/costs by reducing managerial headcount, and to maintain good decision-making by "empowering" lower level managers. Ideally, this allows more rapid decision-making, and closer touch with buyers and the market. Of course, in many cases, companies trade off $70,000-a-year staff positions for loss of multi-million-dollar market positions. The trade-off is not beneficial for the company, middle management, or customers.[14] Management is a valuable function when done properly. Proponents of delayering are often third parties such as consultants, whose performance is not measured by the long-term results/consequences – no matter what they say. This is unethical.

Of course, not all projects require elaborate evaluation and reporting. At one leading consultancy,[15] all evaluations were performed by a third party. That way, the manager who assigned a project could not escape blame.

Naturally, there are miniscule projects which do not warrant much attention at all. These are usually identified through employee morale appraisals, where low morale typically means something is perceived as unfair. Learning how to construct and read these appraisals is an important management tool to identify unethical behavior. This includes maintaining suggestion/comment boxes. Sadly, such direct and unstructured communications are increasingly relics of the past.

---

[13]Rob: in my work as a consultant, I have found generally that the department which sets rewards and compensation is more guarded, and less willing to answer questions than any other.

[14]H. Minzberg, "Musings on Management," *Harvard Business Review*, July–August 1996. One reason that this does happen is that the revenue hit is delayed compared to the cost saving. Management is usually very oriented to the present budget cycle.

[15]Booz, Allen & Hamilton, Inc. (now Strategy&).

With a little finesse, top management should be able to understand and respond to ethical (and other) concerns voiced by employees. In many cases, however, a complaint does not resonate with top management, which frequently is not familiar with the operational or administrative components of the business.

A reduction in force, or an abandonment of past practices such as rotating new hires through on-the-ground functions to learn all aspects of the business, can have disastrous consequences. The Boeing Company, after its 1997 merger with McDonnell Douglas, reduced the number of airplane inspectors dramatically. The result was the 737 MAX crash and loss of life.[16] This violated not just legal standards but also ethical standards. The short-term saving (good) in safety inspectors was more than offset by the later harm. Professor More notes: "The present good must be omitted or reduced from the probable expectation of a future good … more excellent than the present in respect to weight and duration; and therefore much more certain expectations."[17] Retaining a defective management practice is not just a stupid practice, but a dangerous one where the product can threaten lives. A decision to sacrifice safety or quality is usually a violation of ethics, and a poor financial decision by the company.

The recipient of an ethics complaint will not always understand the seriousness of the problem. In those cases, the recipient must put in the requisite time and effort to understand the problem. All too frequently, top management does not want to know about the problem.[18] Ignoring the problem is an abandonment of ethical responsibilities, particularly by the Chief Executive Officer (CEO). While this may avoid legal penalties, the CEO is avoiding his obligation not only to run the company well, but also to be a guiding light for ethical behavior.

This chapter has looked at the role of stupidity in ethical adherence. It shows that stupidity – particularly combined with laziness – is a fertile ground for unethical behavior. As Professor More observes "some [people] are better and more excellent than

[16]DOWNFALL. The Case Against Boeing, Netflix 2022. Rory Kennedy Director.
[17]More, Noema X.
[18]Alvesson, Ibid, pp. 22–23.

others...Wherefore, if any man shall... insist wholly on the delectation of his animal Appetite, he plainly publishes himself for a Brute."[19] Sincerity and effort define the ethical.

The next chapter takes the point of view of top management. Top managers and members of the Board of Directors have control over the ethical direction at a company, and at the same time come face to face with the challenges confronting a company. It looks at the pressures and how top managers can transmit the right ethical directives for the best results.

---

[19]Noema III and Chapter V, Section IV.

SECTION VI

ETHICAL LEADERSHIP

12

ETHICS IN THE BOARDROOM

What is a leader's role in ethics, and what are the obstacles?

Will no one rid me of this meddlesome priest?
                    King Henry II regarding Thomas Becket

Chief Executive Officers (CEOs) have choices. Some are unique to that title, others are shared across the organization. The pressures on a CEO can be more or less intense than on other officers, but the diversity of pressures is unique. The pressures come from various areas, but almost all have consequences for the organization – not in the least, its ethical integrity.

MERGERS AND ACQUISITIONS

Mergers and acquisitions (M&As) can serve many purposes, although they are consistently found to not boost long-term shareholder value.[1] M&As do benefit a narrow group of participants, particularly advisors, investment bankers, accountants, and top management. Often, the board of directors and, in particular, the CEO end up with a huge gain. This is sometimes based on adjusting the CEO's compensation because the new entity is

---

[1] N. Fernandes, "The Value Killers," *Harvard Law School Forum*, on Corporate Governance, January 8, 2020.

bigger.[2] Advisors enthusiastically support these deals because there is a lot of money at stake. For example, when AB InBev merged with SABMiller, advisors collected fees of $1.5 billion. The merger was later described as having "unimpressive" results.[3]

With an army of lawyers, the legality of these transactions is not typically questioned. But are these transactions ethical? Are they moral?

There are arguments on both sides. As the *Financial Times* noted, after a merger, life is often easier for top management.[4] They pick up a lot of money, usually a troublesome competitor is eliminated, and stockholder returns improve.[5] This part of the outcome accords with Noema I, in that it makes their lives "more pleasant and agreeable."[6]

But there are a number of Noemata which do not accord with M&A, depending on whether the longer-term outcomes are positive or negative for consumers. The two guidelines which speak most eloquently against such activity are (1) The stricture against "excess wealth" and (2) the stricture against "cupidity."[7] These two characteristics are inarguably linked to most M&A activity, and so condemn it. Few people would argue that large incomes and greed are not part and parcel of M&A.[8]

---

[2]G. Meeks and J. Meeks, "Mergers Destroy Value. Without Reform, Nothing Will Change," *The Financial Times*, July 20, 2022.
[3]Ibid.
[4]The CEO of a top-three information firm commented that one advantage of M&A is that the analysts could not easily track if she was making progress on promised improvements.
[5]Ibid.
[6]The counterargument is that such mergers can make consumers less well off. The counter-counterargument is that mergers can finance innovation which benefits consumers. These factual outcomes determine whether Noema X which says the present good must be weighed against future good in respect to "weight and duration."
[7]More, Chapter II, Section XII; Chapter 8, Section VII. In particular, cupidity is opposed to gratitude.
[8]See popular descriptions such as T. Wolfe, *Bonfire of the Vanities*, Picador Books, 2008.

COMPANY POLICY

Most companies have thousands, if not tens of thousands of policies and business goals, making it difficult for many new employees to comply and for a board to enforce its will. Fortunately, many corporate/organizational actions are ethical, although not always socially positive.

Below are a list of actual directives and policy questions that we have accumulated over a number of years from a wide range of companies. Some are ethical, but do not create an ethical culture or goodwill. Some are unethical. In the examples below, we have noted those which violate Professor More's principles. Unless we have missed some rules, the others should be ethical – applying the legal principle that "everything which is not illegal must be legal."

Examples vis-à-vis Commercial Policy

Starting with some actions which will not create goodwill, either inside the company or outside of it:

- *We need to find 2–3% more revenue without increasing any direct cost. What do our customer contracts allow us to do other than straightforward price increase?*

- *We need to lower churn. How can we make it more difficult for customers to leave us?*

- *We want to commercially (re)use customer data/metadata. How can we ensure that our Terms and Conditions small print allow us to do this without creating big fuss. . .?*

- *We're losing money/only make very low margins on ABC customer segment (size or geography). How can we lose these customers without being perceived as rude?*

- *Once customers have chosen our solution, they'll have no choice but to select and accept following add-on charges. How can we do this without being perceived as predatory?*

- *Can we invite these specific customers to the Super Bowl Game and spend two days with them?*

Arguably, none of these actions represent best practices. However, there is no clear violation of Noemata or other ethical rules. Of course, how they are executed may change that assessment. What this conclusion and these examples suggest is that ethics does not mean being "nice" or pleasant. There may be reasons *other* than ethics for avoiding these hard-knuckle practices. There can be rewards for good behavior, especially in close-knit industries.

Examples vis-à-vis Partnerships Policy

- *How can we end up demonstrably better off within the partnership than the other side?*

- *"If we see the first signs of success, how can we convert this partnership into a first step toward a friendly merger or a hostile take-over?"*

- *However it works, we should exclusively own the customer contact relationship.*

- *Let's make sure we own the IP and not share it.*

- *The partnership will give us excellent insights into why this party is so successful, and then we can cancel and go it alone.*

The last example is a clear case of an ethical violation. If a partnership is a form of trusting relationship, this [9] violates More's principles of veracity, fidelity, and candor.

Examples vis-à-vis Suppliers' Policy

- *We need to improve our working capital ratio. What can we do to delay paying our suppliers by 45 days?*

---

[9]Chapter VI, Section I.

- *Bank covenants will be calculated based on balance sheet of last day of this quarter. How much of accounts payable can we push into next quarter without getting into legal trouble?*

- *Suppliers cannot put through annual price increases greater than 80% of official inflation % and after adjusting their prices by 3% efficiency improvement.*

- *We need to tell this vendor that we need to always have better conditions than our direct competitor.*

- *Suppliers should upload their invoices into our ERP system, and then we'll pay them after 105 days while deducting a 6% early payment discount, regardless of their terms.*

The last example is not ethical. While some of the previous ones are odoriferous, they do not actually recommend breaking an agreement. The last example appears to be a direct instruction to violate an existing agreement. This violates Professor More's principles for sincerity (Second Book, Chapter III) and cupidity.

Examples vis-à-vis Employees' Policy

- *There's no need to target compensation higher than 50th percentile of our industry.*

- *We need to carry out this reduction-in-force/lay-offs before December 31st so that there will be no need to pay out any accrued bonuses.*[10]

- *Jones would be perfect candidate for this position and in reality is entitled to it, but if we hire him we're going to create a problem in his current department.*

- *All airline frequent flier miles accrued on a business trip should go into the company's account and not the individual employee's.*

---

[10]Very common in the advertising industry.

- *We need to make sure we have the right diversity mix of candidates invited for an interview, rather than ensuring the right diversity mix of employees.*

- *We need to cut business travel cost by 20% across the company, but not for the CEO who must fly first class or by private jet.*

- *Let's interview a number of employees or ex-employees of our principal competitor for a fake or real position and see what we can find out about their company's plans.*

The last situation is a fraud based on a lie. This violates the virtue of veracity (Chapter VI, section I.) In addition, Professor More comments: "There is no quicksand, or infected Air, more frightful to the Traveler, nor any Wizard more dangerous to be met withal than an accomplished Lyar." (Chapter VI, section II)

Examples vis-à-vis Shareholders Policy

- *We can achieve or exceed financial target for this year by not backfilling any open positions including sales rep positions. But this will cause trouble achieving next years' financial targets.*

- *Yes, selling division ABC would yield big earning/share bump, but it will worsen our portfolio of activities versus competition.*

- *We could cut R&D budget by 50% for the duration of the recession.*

- *We should make allowances for these financial misses with regard to executive bonus program as we may lose valuable people, including myself if we don't.*

- *While I agree that the asking price for this acquisition is too high, we need to consider the consequences of not buying this company and watch our competitor do so.*

- *As you can see from the attached report by PWC, buying a private jet will enable me and my executive team to be 15% more productive.*

- *I know that lowering our profits by 15% for the next six quarters will not be acceptable, but if we do we could increase them by 30% thereafter.*

- *If the Board does not want to extend my contract beyond my mandatory retirement age of 65, we should sell the company as it will be impossible to find a good successor. Believe me.*

- *Let's buy this annoying pesky startup and close it down/let's buy this competitor, bamboozle the DOJ (Department of Justice), and then close it down (Oracle vs. Siebel).*

Except for the last example, it is not clear to us that these policy proposals necessarily violate ethical rules. If, as it seems, "bamboozle the DOJ" means breaking rules of disclosure, then it is unethical. Noema XX says: "It is good to obey a magistrate in minor matters, even without fear of punishment." With that in mind, all shareholder rights need be observed.

What to do in circumstances related to the above policy suggestions – and whether they merit a thorough ethics consideration – is an ongoing question for management. Often, pressure from the CEO or the company culture created by the CEO pushes managers to come up with more aggressive, more creative or bolder ways to operate.

The CEO is often acting in response to:

- Pressure from shareholders (direct or via equity analysts) and their wishes vis-à-vis profitability.

- Executive compensation outlook based on company performance outlook.

- Direct response to perceived changes in competitor activities.

- Testosterone and/or personal ethics culture which often can have negative influence on CEO actions and thereby company's well-being.

ROLES

Often employees/managers may also resort to questionable ethics/ greedy actions not in direct response to explicit CEO requests but based on how they interpret a CEO's unspoken wishes or "wink and nod." In bigger companies, CEO wishes/preferences are handed down through multiple management layers and often lose context in translation. A company's general counsel will advise the CEO on what actions could be viewed as illegal, but what is greedy or ethically questionable is not generally within the counsel's scope of advice. It would be highly unlikely for employees to tell a CEO that his suggestions were greedy/unethical.

WHAT TO DO?

So, what can we do about existing greed, particularly if we do not know the source? There are a number of strategies which can help fend off the proponents of greedy pricing. We are not pressing a moral agenda, but are noting that we live in ecosystems (the "garden" of Chapter 1.) which are willing to use means some would describe as greedy. That greed may not be a path which results in loyal customers or longer-term revenue. If you wish to thwart greedy actions, you need to recognize the tactics used. Then businesses and customers might:

- Have advanced tools and measures (shown as a cloud, in Fig. 12.1 below) to show the harm in some greedy tactics. In this way, management will know the sequence of the harm.

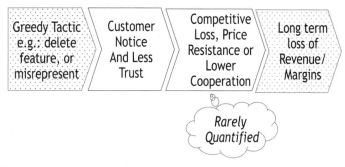

Fig. 12.1. Assessment of Greedy Actions.

Few companies or marketers have reliable links among the steps. Few have really quantified the value of the ancillary service quality. How long does it take customers to respond when, for example, 5% of the market value of a good or service is removed, but the price remains the same? What channel events happen after the change in price/value? What is the lifetime Net Present Value (NPV) of such a move? Without provable benchmarks, the decision will be up to whoever is in power within the firm. The more ethical players may not always win.

- Make incentives include long-term results. There are many ways a smart manager with the wrong motivation can succeed in the short term, but leave chaos in later years.[11] Fortunately, there are early warning signs of greed, such as lack of candor about proposed actions.

- Monitor competitors more closely. In many competitive industries, the competitors may be the ones who will notice short-term impacts first. Their actions, if called out, may be a good early-warning signal if the market frowns. The market will often punish poor behavior – for example, creating extra customer accounts hurt Wells Fargo, and violating privacy at Facebook has led to user hesitancy.[12]

- Preemptive ethics and transparency. This has worked well, both for signals to the market and signals internally. One leading soft drink company got a package containing confidential competitor research on new products and potential pricing being undertaken by its primary competitor. The package was sent by an employee of the competitor. The soft drink company immediately returned the information, unread, to the competitor. The message was clear: only honest competition would be countenanced.

---

[11]Cf. P. Volker, "Think More Boldly," *The Wall Street Journal*, December 14, 2009.
[12]B. Eisen, Wells Fargo Reaches Settlement with Government over Fake-Accounts Scandal, *Wall Street Journal*, February 20, 2021.

ETHICAL STRATEGY[13]

Rarely does management have time to conduct an exhaustive review (to "boil the ocean") looking for unethical behavior (Fig. 12.2, part A), and so managers must know *where to look*.[14]

Perhaps, the best way to encourage ethical behavior is to build an ethical culture. With the right culture, it is more likely that employees will notice unethical actions and act accordingly. But for that to happen, most or all employees need to be part of the ethical culture and that can take 18 months or more.

The alternative to relying on building a culture is to rely on rules. However, relying on rules is often inadequate because there are too many types of marketing and pricing initiatives and because these rules work only under certain circumstances or contexts. If the task

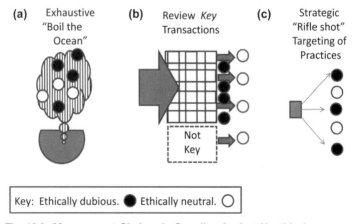

(a) Exhaustive "Boil the Ocean" **(b)** Review *Key* Transactions **(c)** Strategic "Rifle shot" Targeting of Practices

Key: Ethically dubious. ● Ethically neutral. ○

Fig. 12.2. Management Choices in Guarding Against Unethical Practices.

---

[13]The classic McKinsey definition of strategy works well here. Strategy is an integrated set of management (or personal) actions leading to a lasting advantage.

[14]Almost all major companies have a vast array of product variants, and service many different markets. This makes "boiling the ocean" close to impossible. There are many forms of the pricing.

of ferreting out violations of rules is left to top management and the legal department, the number of violations will not be curtailed (Fig. 12.2, part B).

On the other hand, if management knows precisely what the ethical threats are, it can counter them effectively. This is why our outline of greedy tactics/strategies is helpful. This enables top management to ask the right questions, to make sure the right screens are in place, and to have a strategy for stopping unethical actions before they start (Fig. 12.2, part C). This is the most strategic ethical approach.

Approaches A and B may work, but are less effective and efficient than C.

CASE EXAMPLES

An example of the evolution of management behavior can be found by examining a leading manufacturer of Aerial Work Platforms (AWPs), also known as "cherry pickers." The salesforce had become proficient in switching allowable discount amounts from one account to another. In this fashion, a sales person could exceed the allowed account discount set by finance. This was a violation of their condition of employment and so, in the absence of any overarching contrary principles, was unethical.

In addition to excessive discounting, this practice also made it difficult to penetrate new market segments via discounting since intended discounts were transferred to accounts that the salesforce felt comfortable with. When the huge differential in discounts across accounts became public knowledge, customers were angered and went elsewhere.

Management was aware of this practice, but had no idea of its extent. Because management believed the practice was infrequent, it did not want to punish random sales people. Management was reluctant to spend great effort to correct the behavior. The abuse ended only after the AWP manufacturer installed a new accounting system which tracked cash discounting. The shell game ended abruptly.

The benefits were apparent. There was a 5–7% increase in revenues. Customers were no longer outraged to discover discounts of much as 40% to others and not them. And sales people were educated on more scientific bases for discounting. This process took about 18 months.

A CHIEF ETHICS OFFICER

One approach used by a number of companies such as Target, Salesforce.com, Boeing, and others is to appoint a Chief Ethics Officer (also called a Chief Trust Officer). They operate on different charters, including one which is "To develop a strategic framework for the ethical and humane use of technology." The Chief Ethics Officer has a variety of reporting relationships, often CEO or CFO.[15]

The key decision in designing the function is what ethical issues to target. Are they the large collection of line practices, some identified in this Chapter? Or are they matters which have reached the board? In part, this shapes what the ideal manager's credentials will include. We believe that some connection with ethical theory, moral practices, and legal rules is important. But, there is the need to have an officer who can understand the increasingly complex unethical practices at a line level. Many will not detect – or know how to prevent – the unethical strategies mentioned in Chapters 1 and 13. This means that their company will not address some ethical issues until they blow up because they are not recognized. These include pricing and information technology, which are often not familiar to top managers. This is likely to grow to a larger problem as pricing and information technology, e.g., AI, grow in sophistication and use.

Sometimes, a good business financial calculation is important to fight unethical decisions. In 1970, an internal memo was said to have circulated to top Ford management. It was reported that the memo estimated that there would be 180 burn deaths and 180 serious burn injuries in Pintos without fuel tank modifications. It

---

[15]"Rise of the Chief Ethics Officer," *Forbes*, March 27, 2019.

estimated that this would cost Ford $200,000 per death, and in total would cost $50 million.[16]

After long delays, the National Highway Traffic Safety Administration (NHTSA) found that at least 100, and possibly 848 people, burned to death. For liability, courts awarded up to $1.28 million per person.[17] A grossly mistaken estimate, not even considering damage to reputation. A good ethics officer would have challenged the initial estimates, and used better financial and outcome estimates to persuade the board to correct the problem. As is often the case, poor financial skills and poor judgment reinforced a drive to the unethical. If done properly, an ethics officer would have been able to stop the unethical process from the beginning. Note that preventing the problem would have cost $6 per vehicle.

What is clear is that the ability to spot and prevent greed and unethical behavior from the top is usually difficult. Top management must exercise effort to ensure policies are ethical and that an ethical culture is enforced.

---

[16]"The Pinto Memo: 'Its Cheaper to Let Them Burn'," *The Spokesman Review*, Friday, October 17, 2008.
[17]L. Kramer, "Ford Ignored Safety, Prosecution Says," *The Washington Post*, January 10, 1980.

13

SUCCESS THROUGH ETHICS

Question: Are you smart enough to fight a lack of ethics in others, on your own terms?

No Captain can do very wrong by placing his ship alongside the enemy.

Vice Admiral Horatio Nelson

Conducting oneself ethically is the best way to foster a long-term profitable relationship. Ethics are the antecedent building block to establish trust and loyalty. Comparing the "World's Most Ethical Companies" survey to the S&P 500 over time suggests that ethical behavior is rewarded. The most ethical companies outperform other similar-sized companies by 7.1% over a 15-year period.[1] There is considerable evidence that ethical behavior improves customer relationships.[2]

Ethical practices, such as ethical pricing, are a very pragmatic way to build a customer relationship. It means pricing bounded by ethical rules. The rules, some reviewed here, are quite specific. Compared to other management guidelines like Net Promoter

---

[1]Ethisphere Institute "2021 World's Most Ethical Companies" Recognition Program, *Ethisphere*, February 23, 2021.
[2]L. F. Thornton, "Ethics and Trust are Reciprocal," Leading in Context, June 18, 2014. Also O. Ferrell, J. Fraedrich and L. Ferrell, *Business Ethics* (11th Edition), Cengage Learning 2017, p. 16.

Scores (NPSs), they are very concrete and intuitive.[3] NPSs are aggregations of many factors, and while NPS can identify specific contact points which are driving high or low scores, NPS does not identify the key driver of price in that market.

HIGHER STANDARDS

Ethics is about doing good for *all* parties over the long term.[4] While the topic of ethics is broad, there are some clear rules which may be usefully followed in conjunction with an understanding of when and how some people will break the rules. Knowing when and how to guard against ethical breaches in pricing can be called "Strategic Ethical Pricing."[5]

The idea that ethical guidelines are relevant to business success is not new.[6] However, ethical understanding is one thing. Actual practice is another. It is important to understand your opposition and counter unethical behaviors with your strengths.[7] This is how corporate top management can efficiently ensure compliance to ethics.

There are several benefits to adhering to a higher ethical standard. For one, it can mean higher revenues. This raises the question: "What is the ethical standard?" As most readers will know by reference to Chapter 9, there are many articulations of ethical standards and the focus of ethics has varied over the years. However, some of the basic principles remain unchanged. Using the list of standards published by Professor More suggests what guidelines management might use to demonstrate ethical integrity to their customers and partners. (See Appendix.)

---

[3]A popular business tool which claims to measure customer sentiment.

[4]R. Cudworth, Law of Nature, *Encyclopedia Britannica*, 11th Edition, p. 829.

[5]E. V. Lopez, "Strategic Ethics and Governance," BizStrategy, 2017, Singapore. Dr Lopez observes that corporations set ethical standards to meet goals, either for profit for to fit corporate cultural goals. This book is consonant with that thesis.

[6]J. Ewing, "Can a Company Be Virtuous and Profitable?" *The New York Times*, November 17, 2019, p. BU1.

[7]C. von Clausewitz, *Clausewitz on Strategy*, Chapter on Attack and Defense, p. 109, J. Wiley & Co. (2001).

The failure to accord with Noemata, essentially ethical failures, leads to business reverses. Some examples of principles and corporate result from several perspectives:

Quality of Service	*Principle:* Live by promises.[8]
	Example: A leading systems developer rolled out a new billing system for telecom providers in the United States and Canada. However, the $65 million system did not function according to specifications. In Canada, the system was sold to Bell Canada Mobility. After attempts to fix the system failed, the developer abandoned the project. Bell Canada cancelled the contract and communicated the failure to all telecoms and other leading businesses in Canada. In the next year, the systems developer was forced to close all but one of its Canadian offices as its customer base collapsed based on the Bell Canada experience. In the United States, however, sales continued for over two years.
	Management actions: In the United States, the developer had gotten away with the failures, as customers did not communicate with one another. Management failed to address the problem. As a result, there was a material revenue contraction in Canada.
	Ideal Management Strategy: Work to stand behind promises and product. A good example is LEGO's customer satisfaction policies, which contribute to its position as the world's most valuable toy brand.[9]
	Benefit: Many markets reward high quality of service or product. If the developer had secured Bell Canada Mobility as a satisfied client, it would have locked in that client for another five years and gained at least three more Canadian telecoms as clients.
	Risks: Risks of standing behind the product would

---

[8]Ibid. Noemata IV and V. (bad is measured by comparison to the good, and bad is remembered longer.)
[9]"Lego's Solid Foundations Stack up as World's Most Valuable Toy Brand." Brand Finance, Report 25, 2019. Similarly M. Solomon "How LEGO Customer Service Wins Back Upset Customers: A Simple Recovery Approach Works Wonders," Forbes.com, April 13, 2018. This gives an example of LEGO customer service.

Typical Ethical Project Schedule

Understand	Plan	Launch	Execute
• Ethical goals • Broad survey of corp. practices • Key market issues • Internal view/ resistance • Market segments and wants	• Cost/benefit (by segment) • Implementation costs and risks • Focus of initiative • Champions and oversight • Mngt team briefing	• Go/No Go • Guidelines • Broader internal communication • Measures of impact on revenues and ethics • Rewards	• Milestones • Hold individuals responsible • Legal reviews • Adjustments • Results • Other foci in business?

• *No trials*
• Not consensus based

Fig. 13.1. Typical Ethical Pricing Project Schedule.

include costs of further development, and complaints of delay, with perhaps adverse effects in the market.

Context

Principle: A lack of clarity in principles results in confusion and customer greed reduces revenues.[10]
Example: A leading legal service provider which worked on retainer knew that some smaller companies were listing the legal service provider as their representative, but in fact they were not connected and paid no fees for the representation.
Rationale for behavior: Managers were trained to strictly observe procedures for signing new clients, and so felt they could not bill the self-listing clients for the service.
Ideal Management Strategy: If the provider had been clear on fair exchange of benefits and payments, the customers would have been billed immediately upon listing the provider as their representative.
Benefit: The service provider billed approximately 40,000 self-service clients and added over $3.1 million to revenues.
Risks: The risks to encouraging workers to go

[10]H. More, *Enchiridion Ethicum, praecipua Moralis Philosophiae Rudimenta complectens, illustrate ut plurimum Veterum Monument, 1667. Noema XII (how the bad obscures moral principles).*

beyond normal routines is real, but can be countered through effective communication up and down the chain of command.

Mis-Representation	*Principle:* Treat customers candidly. Be sincere. Share issues with them.[11]

Example: A leading tax service provider found that a competitor was materially undercutting published prices and standard industry rates. The provider experienced a slow erosion of its most profitable clients who defected to obtain lower prices.

Rationale for behavior: Tax provider did not want to alert customers that there were price variations, for fear of provoking questions of its own pricing.

Ideal Management Strategy: Management contacted the competitor's older best customers and let them know that other, new customers were obtaining a much lower price. This incensed the older customers who complained to the competitor.

Benefit: The competitor ceased undercutting prices immediately. While none of the angry customers defected, several extracted deep rebates. No further defections occurred.

Risks: There was some risk of a broader price war, but this did not happen as it was to neither provider's benefit.

Bullying Customers	*Principle:* Do not bully, ambush, or lock in clients.[12]

Example: During the 2000s, a leading internet service provider set its pricing to retain customers. There were penalties for cancellation outside a narrow time band, and alternating periods of limited and unlimited usage, which led users to incur excess usage charges.

Rationale for behavior: This pioneering internet service provider, a dial-up, was facing rapid share loss as broadband and lower-priced providers entered

---

[11]Ibid. Noema XIII, 3 (importance of sincerity).
[12]Ibid. Noemata XV and XXIII (refrain from doing injury, or you will lose rights to past acquisitions).

the market. Management compensation depended on retaining customers. Many subscribers were not adept at exiting.

Ideal Management Strategy: Management should have addressed the problem, particularly in the face of overwhelming subscriber hostility. It should have updated its technology rapidly to retain older subscribers.

Benefit: As a result of a focus on retaining its existing client base through penalties and other ambush tactics, the provider failed to develop alternatives under consideration, such as nationwide wireless service ("WiMAX") which might have given it renewed leadership and revenue gains.

Risks: Sometimes pursuing a "harvest" strategy can produce the most profits for a company (for example, mainframe computing and print photography), and simply riding the existing technology and customer base might have been the best shareholder (if not management) option.[13]

Embedding	*Principle:* Integrity brings benefit.[14]

Example: In 2007, Coca Cola Company received an envelope from an employee at a competitor containing information regarding the competitor's product development programs and market focus. Coca Cola immediately sealed the envelope and sent it back to the competitor's management and included the name of the employee who had sent it.

Rationale for behavior: Coca Cola did this as a reflection of its ethical culture. It also was confident it could succeed in the market without using a competitor's confidential information.

Ideal Management Strategy: Coca Cola did exactly the right thing.

Benefit: This action reinforced its world-class reputation and set an example for employees.

---

[13]Eastman Kodak saw it net revenue and ROI improved from 2005 to 2017. *Macrotrends* January 2022.
[14]Ibid. Noema XIV (do good, as you would want it done to you).

	Risks: Sometimes success depends on learning the other side's secrets.
Discrimination not reflecting costs	*Principle:* Show fairness and social equity to all.[15] *Example:* In some cases, buyer perception of the seller's brand is linked to a broader, perhaps controversial, conflict, such as gender, race, age, politics, nationalism, or rights such as abortion or gun possession. For instance, auto insurance pricing for males runs about 14% higher than the same insurance for similarly situated females. Of course, it should be higher based on accident rate differentials which cost insurers more. However, suppose costs for female services and products are higher? Indeed, many services and products bear a "pink tax" and are priced higher for women than for men. Average prices of haircuts and laundry services, for example, are higher, although these may reflect higher costs or women's preferences for higher quality.[16] *Benefit:* Either costs or differential positions of customers may prompt differences in price, but sometimes management may underestimate the long-lasting harm from price discrimination.[17] *Risks:* Some fear that failure to reflect cost differentials may harm profitability. Note that often, costs were not properly examined. For example, Colonial Penn found that elderly drivers were lower cost because they drove fewer miles and so used price to become the leader in the senior automobile owner market.[18]

---

[15]Ibid Noema XIX (no one should live a bountiful life while others live calamitously).

[16]When Brooks Brothers moved from selling only men's apparel, they discovered that women returned and exchanged purchases more frequently than typical male customers. There was also more rapid evolution in styles.

[17]See K. Roose "The Staying Power of an Uproar," *The New York Times*, February 1, 2022 p. B1.

[18]R. Metz, "Market Place; Colonial Penn: What Next?" *The New York Times*, July 22, 1981.

STUPID DISCRIMINATION

The last principle suggests a basic management truism. There is often no reason to base differential pricing on race or gender – they are crude screens.[19] Generally, there are more sophisticated behavior criteria. For instance, rather than differentiate car repair prices based on gender, it is much more effective to base them on the history of car ownership and prior repairs. This will distinguish the price-insensitive from the knowledgeable who may not be able to evaluate costs. Doing this by gender – especially in an age of social media – may generate anger and backlash.

If only one identifiable group has been subject to a unique set of factors, it can be easy for marketing managers to reach confident conclusions regarding potential actions. But this is almost never the case. For instance, confronted with low Net Promoter Scores, many line managers simply undertake the program they wanted to execute anyhow and say – usually incorrectly – that it will cure the low score in the market.[20]

IMPLEMENTATION

How to implement an ethical pricing program? A key question is who will be the champion of such a program? It may take some effort to convince some managers that ethics increases profitability. Some market-facing managers who have obtained short-term revenue hikes from unethical actions may be uninterested in the longer-term consequences. In other cases, there may be unethical actions which, while highly annoying to customers, are important to a small budget. For instance, a shift from billing via USPS to online-only has a 2%–20%+ impact on billing operations, or less

---

[19]Clearly some differences among customers do become visible at the demographic level. R. Smith, "Retailers Tackle an Online Gender Gap," *The New York Times*, March 14, 2008, and C. Pittman, "Black Men and Women Spend more on Apparel. Race, Social Context and Consumption: How race structures the consumption preferences and practice of Middle and Working Class Blacks," Doctoral dissertation, Harvard University.
[20]There was a joke in the British military in World War II. It said "First, you fire your gun. Then, if it hits anything, you say that was your target."

than 1%–5% of total costs, but this may alienate buyers who are not computer facile.

Ethics-based initiatives differ from general marketing initiatives in that there should be *no trials* regarding ethical value. Trials suggest that the company has some doubt about whether an ethical practice is the right path. The use of a trial leaves open the possibility that the company could, in effect, say: "Oops! I guess we won't be ethical in that way!" Trials are acceptable as long as they are clearly operational trials, such as testing out a new supervisory approach.[21]

An ethical pricing trial cannot be a consensus-based process. There must be complete confidence in the ethics. The vast majority of employees look for strong leadership from top management in dealing with ethical issues.[22]

Institutionally, it is worth distinguishing management roles. As the chief financial officers (CFOs) at two banks observed, some "C" titles are inclined to defend the institution (CFO or Chief Counsel, for example) while others are more focused on short-term revenue (CEO, Head of sales, and product management).[23] In general, the more institutionally oriented management will be more willing to make a short- versus long-term trade-off in migrating to more ethical practices, and so may be the better initial champions of these efforts.[24] Later, after the practices are successfully established, the leadership efforts might be taken up by revenue-oriented titles.

For many companies, the notion that ethics may be a powerful driver of annual revenues is a novel concept. For some, this is a foundation for longer-term growth. In fact, all may benefit from applying ethical rules broadly.

This chapter has taken a line management overview of ethics and corporate operations. It shows that ethical initiatives require careful planning and skill. Understanding unethical and greedy actions is necessary to ensure that ethical standards prevail.

---

[21]Based on consulting case experience.
[22]19th Annual Edelman Trust Barometer, October–November, 2018. See p. 21 on leadership.
[23]Interview with North American Development Bank CFO Julio Zamora, December 15, 2021.
[24]Interviews with two CFOs at leading banks 2016–2020.

14

ETHICS AND THE APOCALYPSE

Question: Can I Afford to be Ethical in Bad Times?

> If we still have time, we might just get by
> Every time I think about it, I want to cry.

Heart

Thanks to motion pictures and television, we are all familiar with the idea of a catastrophic end of civilization. In these dramatizations, we see how, during an apocalypse, fellow humans react badly, selfishly, and unethically.

But is that a true portrait? Obviously, we have no direct experience with the end of the world. However, we do know of experiences that occurred at a time when most humans probably were sure that the world was ending.

Looking at the years 536–540 AD, survival was not the obvious outcome to those living at the time. Three events destroyed much of civilization and caused countless deaths. These were:

- The final collapse of the Roman Empire. Rome's fall to barbarian tribes meant that the *Pax Romana* had ceased to exist. The barbarian tribes were free to raid cities and seize agricultural goods and people. Many cities were abandoned.

- A seemingly mysterious fog plunged Europe, the Middle East, and parts of Asia into darkness, day and night, for 18 months.

In fact, this fog was the result of cataclysmic volcanic eruptions in 536–540 AD. The eruptions turned the sky dark and gray, and caused widespread deaths of plants and animals for much of two years.

- This period of darkness is now thought to have promoted the spread of the plague – the Justinian bubonic plague killed 35–55% of the population. Annoyed by the darkness, infected fleas reacted to the darkness by biting – and infecting – humans.[1] This massive die-off caused the collapse of institutions and further abandonment of cities.

LIFE AT A BAD MOMENT

An apocalypse brings fear, harm, dangers, and death. Additionally, an apocalypse narrows one's time horizons. An investment horizon is the length of time an investor is planning to maintain their portfolio. That, in turn, is determined by risk.[2] While fleeing masses were probably not thinking about their portfolios that way, they were surely focused on the immediate or the short term. Roman

---

[1] A more formal statement of the problem: "Ultimately, the cold rainy weather, or more probably droughts followed by such weather, brought a population explosion among Yersinia carriers such as the African gerbil. These rodents were forced out from their normally enclosed ecosystem in Northeastern Africa in an effort to feed their ever-increasing numbers. This brought them into contact with the *Rattus rattus*, a rodent that has evolved into an almost symbiotic relationship with human beings. The parasitic hitchhiker, *Xenopsylla cheopis*, unable to feed itself due to the *Yersinia pestis* bacillus, jumped desperately from rat to human at a frenetic pace." And so spreading the bacillus. R. Bilich, "Climate change and Great Plague Pandemics of History: Causal Link between Global Climate Fluctuations and Yersinia Pestis Contagion?" University of New Orleans Theses and Dissertations. 632 (2007), p. 13.

[2] See James Chen, "What is an investment time horizon?" Investopedia, July 30, 2021.

statesman Cassiodorus reported at the time that due to massive crop failures, people had to rely on stored foods to survive.[3]

In addition to the shortening of time horizons, there is likely to have been a lack of concern for the truth of what was going on.[4] Finally, the lack of communication with the rest of the world probably led survivors to believe they had come out best.[5]

The picture which emerges of peoples' mindset during these catastrophic years is that of small groups of people, each focused on short-term survival, and each believing that they did a better job of surviving than other groups. (In some cases, where the other groups died off, this was true, but the belief was general.) Importantly, the interests of the small groups were placed ahead of broader interests.[6]

Given this context, it appears that surviving groups were likely to have had a very strong belief in their group practices. They likely believed that they held the key to survival. This may have included some practices which are not viewed as good, but were necessary, such as ruthless scavenging. Any evaluation of the practices at the time was likely very short term and not particularly based on ethics. For example, during the Roman Empire, violence was prevalent, including the assassination of opponents because of disagreements or to obtain assets, such as farmland and weapons. It was a time of tumult and fear.[7]

Out of this emerged King Leovigild, one of the most powerful Visigoth rulers at that time, who oversaw the building of cities in an

---

[3]T. Hodgkin, *The letters of Cassiodorus*, University of California Press; First edition (September 8, 2020), pp. 518–520.

[4]See D. Effron, "Why Trump Supporters Don't Mind His Lies," *New York Times*, April 29, 2018. Prof. Effron of London Business School notes that "Even if they know the claims are false, they can imagine how they *could* have been true."

[5]M. Fabrykant, V. Magun, "Contrasting perspectives: Belief in national superiority in relation to countries' performance," *International Journal of Comparative Sociology*, August 2022.

[6]M. S. Bjornlie, *The Selected Letters of Cassiodorus*, University of California Press, 2020. Examples include letter from Theodosius concerning local groups taking pastureland from the Imperial mail system, maintenance of aqueducts and of walls. pp. 174–186.

[7]E. J. Watts, *Mortal Republic. How Rome Fell into Tyranny*, Basic Books, 2022.

era when many cities were being abandoned.[8] Leovigild built the strongest kingdom in the post-Roman world with unprecedented (for barbarian) legal and tax systems. This was an effective response to the chaos, and his was apparently an ethical reign.[9] This tells us that abandoning ethics was not a key to success in this stressful time. In fact, we can infer from Leovigild's success as an ethical leader, that ethics was helpful, even then.

ETHICS IN 536 AD

Violent and desperate groups fighting for survival and a better life would recognize few of the Noema outlined by Professor More. At best, they might observe two Noemata:

- The present is the primary concern (Noema VIII).

- The present situation would be tolerated, in order to avoid the probability that future evil is infinitely greater (Noema XI).

Probably of lesser interest to those who lived past 536 AD are several Noema which could have ameliorated the situation. These are:

- To learn about differentials in happiness and success among groups, such as how to grow food in lower-light conditions, and defend farms from warriors (Noema IV and VI).

- The present good must be reduced from the expectation of future good, e.g., maintaining reserves such a seed reserves (Noema X).

- Whatever good you wish to be done to you in the given circumstances, you must do the same to another (Noema XIV).

- It is good and just that everyman's use and possession may be permitted without molestation (Noema XXII).

---

[8]J. Urbanus, "The Visigoth's Imperial Ambitions," *Archaeology*, March/April 2021, pp. 50–55.
[9]Ibid, p. 52.

These four rules would have expedited the transition from the worst of 536 AD to the relatively better ages that followed. For instance, the trade of goods – required, for example, because metal for tools and weapons were not homogenously distributed – would have emerged more quickly, with accompanying increases in wealth.[10] With the return of peace replacing raids and warfare, which damaged crops, food would have become more abundant.

RELEVANCE

But are ethics relevant to an apocalypse? After all, during an apocalypse there is little building of relationships, nor of community, nor of civilization and standards. The overall good of society seems less relevant because it is about to end.

Yet, when life may appear bleak and short-lived, we see positive actions parallel ethical rules. Taking a more recent example of extreme conditions, at the Battle of Stalingrad, the Axis experienced casualty rates above 80%, and the Soviets experienced almost 50% casualties. This, and the horrendous physical conditions, may well have felt apocalyptic. But, as mentioned *supra*, German and Soviet troops traded water and cigarettes at close quarters in 1942/1943.[11]

What can we learn from studying the events which, at the time, may have felt like the world was ending? We believe that theoretically,[12] observing more ethical rules would have benefited the remnants of the Roman Empire in Spain.

Perhaps the most important ethical rule, relevant to the survivors, however, is Noema V which dictates that "evil" must be shunned. At this time, the ultimate evil was clear: the bubonic plague. Shunning other groups which showed they had been contaminated would have been a very prudent measure. Refraining from stealing their livestock would be similarly good. This also would have prevented contact with rodents and other flea-bearing vehicles.

---

[10]See, e.g.: M. Piexoto, Trade, Wealth and Exchange in the Middle Ages, University of Oregon, HC-223H.
[11]Merezhko, supra, p. 13.
[12]We ethical theorists like theorizing.

"Evil" in this context is an ethical, not a moral, categorization. Evil in an ethical context reduces human well-being and happiness.[13] It does not require that groups suffering from the plague be bad, only that they bring unhappiness – such as spreading the plague.

Returning to a basic premise of this book: people benefit from ethical behavior, and ethics are a good way to ward off threats and misfortune. Not just during an apparent apocalypse but also today. While some of the ethical strictures may seem ruthless (e.g., do not help groups suffering from the plague) in the long run, these are good strategies for improved lives.

---

[13]Noema II.

APPENDIX

Prof More's laid out his ethical conclusions and Noemata in his 1667 book *Echiridion Ethicum*, which was published in Latin. That content was later released in translation to English in 1690. Some of the content most relevant to this book are mentioned as follows.[1]

Noema I
* It is good that it is acceptable, pleasant, and agreeable to any perceptive life, to the degree of this life, and conjoined with the preservation of the perceiver.

Noema II
But that which is ungrateful, unpleasant, and inappropriate for any person's perceptive life, or that of this degree of life; and if finally conjoined with the destruction of the perceiver, the worst of all.

For example, if anything offended not only the ears or the eyes, but would also induce deafness and blindness, this would be very bad. But it would be an ill-prepared evil, though the sight would only weaken or the hearing would become impaired. The same applies to other faculties.

Noema III
Of the species or degrees of perceptible lives which are found in the universe of things, some are more excellent and more excellent than others.

Noema IV
One good can be more excellent in nature, duration, or both.

This is self-evident. It can, however, be illustrated by this inconvenience,

---

[1] H. More, *Enchiridion Ethicum*, Benjamin Tooke, 1690. The English Translation of 1690, or An Account of Virtue, Dr Henry More's Abridgement of Morals, Put into English, The Facsimile Text Society, 1930.

that one life would not otherwise be more excellent than the other, nor one happiness greater than the other. Therefore, God, Angel, Man, Horse, and any one of the most vile Crimson would be equally happy. Which no one can in any way admit, unless plainly insane. Concerning Duration, even the smallest doubt or difficulty can arise.

Noema V

That which is good must be chosen; but the evil must be shunned; the less we must endure the evil, lest we should undergo the greater.

Noema VI

In that which we ourselves have not yet experienced, we must be believed to those who profess to have experienced, only they live a life conformed to their profession, and no treachery steals away the catch of any worldly advantage.

Noema VII

The absence of the good which is related to eight is more eligible than the presence of the evil which is similar to eight in respect to weight and duration; and yet so much the more eligible, as much as the evil exceeds the good in weight and duration.

Noema VIII

That which is to be certain ought to have the character of the present, as that which will someday in fact occupy us as present as present. And there is an unequal ratio of that which is very probable in the future.

Noema IX

The less outstanding goods are measured by the more excellent as to their weight and duration.

Noema X

The present good must be omitted or reduced from the probable expectation of a future good infinitely more excellent than the present in respect to weight and duration; and therefore much more than certain expectations.

Noema XI

The present evil is to be tolerated, in order to avoid the probability that the future evil is infinitely greater than the present in respect to weight and duration.

Noema XIII

We must pursue the greatest and most perfect Good with the greatest zeal, and lesser Goods with a zeal proportionately less. Nor must we subordinate greater Goods to less, but less to greater.

Noema XII

The free prejudgment of the affections judges the mind more rightly than when it is entangled or disturbed by the impressions of any bodily passions.

For just as the cloudy and stormy sea does not transmit light; the mind is so disturbed and obscured by the passions, that it scarcely admits even the clearest reason. By this similitude Boethius brilliantly illustrates the matter in that poem, "When the stars can shed black clouds no light, &c. It is indeed longer than that it ought to be transcribed here."

3. And these are almost the Noemata which cause prudence, temperance, and fortitude to be engendered in the soul, which pertain to duty toward ourselves. The things that follow look to the duty toward others, think men and God and virtue, and therefore are the foundations of Sincerity, Justice, Gratitude, Mercy, and Compassion. For piety is ranked among the moral virtues, since God is knowable by the light of nature.

Noema XIV

Whatever good you wish to be done to you in the given circumstances, you must do the same to another in the same circumstances, as far as possible without causing injury to any third party.

Noema XV

You ought to refrain yourself from doing that to another, as long as it is possible without injury to any third party.

Noema XVI

Good is to be offenced to the good, not to the evil.

Noema XVII

It is good for a man to have where he lives well and happily.

Noema XVIII

If it is good for one man to have the means to live well and happily, it follows from a certain analogy and plainly mathematical, that it is twice as much better to have two men, three times as three, a thousand times as a thousand, and so on.

Noema XIX

It is better for one man to live not delicacies than the other so calamitous and miserably.

Noema XX

It is good to obey a magistrate in minor matters, even without any fear of punishment.

Noema XXI

It is better to obey God than men in our own desires.

Noema XXII

It is good and just that it be given to each his own, and that his use and possession may be permitted him without molestation.

Noema XXIII

It is, however, clear that a man can behave himself in such a way that what is his acquisition or gift may cease to be his right.

CHAP. VI. OF ACQUIRING THE REDUCTIVE VIRTUES; AND FIRST OF THOSE, WHICH REFER TO JUSTICE

1. Among the Virtues call'd *Reductive*; those more especially shine out, which have reference to Justice: As
   - Liberality,
   - Magnificence,
   - Veracity,
   - Gratitude,
   - Candor,
   - Urbanity,
   - Fidelity,
   - Modesty,
   - Humanity,
   - Hospitality,
   - Friendship,
   - Civility,
   - Affability,
   - Officiousness.

Liberality is not to be neglected: Since, on the one hand, we shew thereby, that our Souls are not contracted to the bare admiration of Wealth; Nor our Minds, on the other hand, so stupid, as not to understand the true Use and Ends thereof.

Magnificence is prais'd by its own works; since these bring Benefit to the Publick, Ornament to the World, and Variety to the Histories of the Time.

2. VERACITY must be our constant Inmate and Companion: For 'tis the worst of Characters to be a noted Lyar. There is no Quicksand, or infected Air, more frightful to the Traveler, nor any Wizzard more dangerous to be met withal, than an accomplish'd Lyar. He will lead you, like a Ghost, into dangerous Paths; and, when you are wandring quite out of your Way, he will be sure to leave you in the Dark.

However, 'tis strange to see how the Masters in this Talent, will yet set up for Men of Prudence. They are indeed wise enough to know that every Vice must bear a virtuous Name; and that Fraud and Cunning, will never stand alone. 'Tis as with Strumpets, who affect to be seen at Church among the Matrons: but as they are the more abhorr'd herein for their Impudence, as well as Vice; so ought it be with these plausible Circumventors. There is even a Sect of these, who also set up for Wits; they think there can be no greater Excellency than in the way call'd *Bantering*: Surely the Man must be very dull, that cannot Deceive, if he but resolve to Lye. Yet as he that will deceive when he can, shews a Mind that is vile and abject: So the truly prudent and generous Man, is he that will be Honest in the dark: He that will be as just, when 'tis in his power to be otherwise, as if it were not. But whoever notes the Events of things shall see, that Knaves and Hypocrites are expos'd to shame, and end their Lives obscurely; whereas the just and vertuous sort endure, and their Reputation still shines forth as at the Noon-day. Every counterfeit thing must be short-liv'd.

Fidelity is much to be cultivated; and how could Human Society consist without it: since to keep Promises, and to restore what is deposited with us, are the top branches and conspicuous parts of *Justice*.

Hence also we may be convinc'd how much it imports us to consider well of Gratitude. For every good turn done us is, as it were a Pledg deposited in our trust and keeping: And surely he that repays it not back, as soon as he can, is guilty of *Infidelity*. Nay, *Gratitude* is so remarkable a part of *Justice*, that whoever has the heart to violate this Bond is thought capable (might he do it with Impunity) of trampling on all the Laws of the World.

Now who would incur this Character, or draw himself under so dismal a Guilt? There is certainly no Monster that a Man should more abhor, than this Monster of *Ingratitude*.

3. As to the shew and expression of *Candor* in our Converse with Men, there are great Motives for it. First, Because the Errors of most Men are Errors of Ignorance: and yet, even among these Errors, their Minds often labor to bring forth Truth and good Works; a Birth which indeed we ought kindly to assist, by interpreting favorably all their Actions, and affording them the very best appearances we can. For we do, by this soft Temper, help on Peace, and the cementing of Men's Minds toward a bond of Unity: which is so worthy a part, that all Men ought to endeavor it.

4. FOR *Urbanity*, we must not be so Morose, as not to hear and bear the Jests of others (and sometimes tart ones too) altho we are not good at Jesting our selves. In truth, he that is dexterous in Raillery, has found a Remedy to laugh away his Labor, and a very good Sauce against the fatigues of Life. For tho it was not Nature's Intention, to fit us only for Sport and Pastime; Yet these, doubtless, are lawful in their seasons, just as sleep, and other Refreshments, to the Body and the Mind: provided always that things of Moment are not obstructed by them. 'Tis to this sense that *Cicero* speaks in his *Offices, That the ways of Jesting are very different: the one, Sawey, Rustic, Impious, and Obscene; the other, Elegant, Candid, Ingenuous, and Pleasant.* And surely, 'tis this last which is recommended to us. However, if something herein should drop, so quick and pleasing to the Company as to cause Laughter for the smart which it reflects; he that feels it (being a good Man) will not so much vex to see, that small defects are insulted over, as have cause to rejoice, that his greater Virtues are at the same time applauded: For he hears the worst that can be said of him, since Adversaries are still known to shoot their longest and sharpest Arrows. And here we refer to what (in our *First Book*) was said of the *Interpretation of Passions;* which may farther illustrate this Point. * But if some rude and ill-natur'd Man shall perhaps bear-over-hard upon us, and both jest and sting together; We must then do what we can, to cure the subject matter, and draw out that Core, in which his Darts are fix'd.

5. MODESTY must attend all our Actions; 'tis the Flower, * the Beauty of *Jesutice*, and even its chief Perfection: This we have already set forth, and it needs not be repeated.

But *Humanity* does challenge a most principal regard among all the other Virtues. We are all, as it were, linked in one common chain of Equality; nor is one man to think himself so very preferable to another; when, in things of Passion and of Reason, in Death and Immortality, we seem all to share alike. He therefore that contemns another, and forgets that way of Treatment, which *Candor* and *Humanity* demands, he seems to give Sentence against himself. For 'twill be as lawful at another time, and when Circumstances are alike, to refuse to him those common Perquisites of Human Nature; seeing in his turn he refused them to others. So that whoever arrogates to himself a great Preeminence above his Fellow-Creatures, does but expose his Vanity, and takes pains to be Ridiculous. Let no man, of how mean a Condition soever, if he be a good Man, and has not by his Follies lost all Title to the Rights of Human Nature, be treated with Contumely. 'Tis the saying of *Heraclitus, Enter, Gentlemen, even here the Gods inhabit*: Which may truly be said of the poorest Man living, so that his Heart be but sound and Just. For (besides that Prerogative, which is common to Mankind) such a one should be regarded with Love and Tenderness, and as it were some Creature that were even Holy and Divine.

6. FOR *Hospitality*, it will stand less in need of Recommendation, as 'tis a manifest part of *Humanity*. It seems to be most needful there, where Strangers are liable to be ill us'd by the Natives, and where they want the things of Accommodation they were us'd to find at Home. These therefore we should strive to Help and Succor, in all they can need at our Hands: Not forgetting that even Holy Angels are thus employ'd, whom we ought to imitate. For they, during this Earthly pilgrimage of our Souls; do seasonably step in, both to relieve and succor us, when we are most distress'd.

7. FOR what concerns *Friendship* and *Friends*, these are carefully to be Acquir'd; and not barely as Ornaments, but as Bulwarks in Human Life. If you light on such as deserve your fervent Love; place it rather on their Virtues, than their Persons, which are both mutable and mortal. Let not your *Friendship* consist, in soft and unprofitable strains; nor in

vehemency of Passion, which would bring many a storm and disorder to your Mind. But let the Character of it be *Sincere* and *Constant*, and such as fulfills all the Duties appertaining thereto, with a chearful and officious Benignity.

8. LASTLY, As to *Civility*, *Affability*, and *Officiousness*; these are all to be regarded, not only as Credentials, which procure us Fame and good Will: but they very often become the very Essential Knots of that Peace and Friendship which we enjoy. Therefore let no Man neglect, and much less despise these smaller Virtues; which often, as smaller Wires, sustain much weight. We do by them live more pleasantly among our Neighbors; our security becomes the greater and our Favor and Credit with Men is there|by increas'd. And who wou'd not wear such things about him, as make him welcom where-e'er he comes, and cost him nothing the Carriage?

CHAP. IX. OF THAT MEDIOCRITY, IN WHICH VERTUE DOES CONSIST: AND OF THE TRUE MEASURE OF SUCH MEDIOCRITY

1. THAT Vertue lies in a *Mediocrity* is not quite untrue, * if rightly understood: Yet as some introduce Vertue attended, on each hand, with opposite Vices; and just as it were a Rose placed between two Nettles: This, we do confess, were a pretty Show, but it cannot possibly hold in every Case.

2. FOR in the Case of *Justice*, where a Man takes no more than what is of right his due; this is plainly opposite to that part which is vicious, and where a Man takes more than what is his due. But here if a Man takes less; this surely seems no Vice, but rather a sort of *Generosity*, or *Modesty*. So again in the Conferring of Rewards, to bestow less than was agreed for, hath as much of *Injustice*, as to give according to Proportion is just: Yet to bestow more largely than was agreed for, is not, on the other hand, *Injustice*, but rather *Liberality*. So also, in the way of Buying and Selling; the overweight that is thrown in to get a Customer's good Will, altho either in Weight or Measure, it exceed the Bargain, yet surely this has nothing of *Injustice* in it.

3. MOREOVER unto *Prudence* (which doubtless is a Moral Vertue) there is only *Imprudence* to be oppos'd, which is the Defect of *Prudence*. So

to *Sincerity* is nothing opposite but *Insincerity*, or at large *Hypocrisie*, which exceeds or falls short of the Perfection of *Sincerity*. So *Patience, Continence,* and *Suffering,* do only go lame (as we say) on the one side, as namely, by *Impatience, Incontinence,* and by *Effeminacy:* So *Temperance* by *Intemperance.* And therefore to put (which some do) a sort of *Insensibility,* to answer as an opposite Vice on the other side, is quite without Reason. F ● ... (as *Andronicus* notes from *Aristotle*) *'tis scarce within Reach of Human Nature to be Insersible to such a Pitch:* And if any Man were so, this would look much more like a Disease of the Body, than a Vice of the Soul.

BUT should it happen, that the Power of the Soul could be so far extended, as to be able to weigh down, and even extinguish the sense of every Corporeal Pain and Pleasure; this certainly were so far from being a Defect in the Soul, that it would rather amount to a wonderful Vertue and Perfection. And to abuse such Perfection would argue either Insincerity, or Imprudence. However, if any Man will needs call it an *Intemperate sort of Temperance,* I will not much contend in the Matter.

END

INDEX